To

_____

From

_____

Date

_____

STORIES TO WARM
A
Grandma's
HEART

True Stories of Hope and Inspiration

EDITED BY JAMES STUART BELL

Guideposts

Stories to Warm a Grandma's Heart

ISBN-10: 0-8249-4501-8
ISBN-13: 978-0-8249-4501-5

Published by Guideposts
16 East 34th Street
New York, New York 10016
Guideposts.org

Scripture references are from the following sources: The New King James Version (NKJV). Copyright © 1982 by Thomas Nelson, Inc. Used by permission. The Holy Bible, New International Version®, NIV®. Copyright © 1973, 1978, 1984, 2011 by Biblica, Inc.™ Used by permission of Zondervan. All rights reserved worldwide. The Holy Bible, New Living Translation (NLT), copyright 1996, 2004. Used by permission of Tyndale House Publishers, Inc., Wheaton, Illinois. *The Message* (MSG). Copyright © 1993, 1994, 1995, 1996, 2000, 2001, 2002 by Eugene Peterson. Used by permission of NavPress, Colorado Springs, CO. All rights reserved.

Distributed by Ideals Publications, a Guideposts company
2630 Elm Hill Pike, Suite 100
Nashville, Tennessee 37214

Guideposts and *Ideals* are registered trademarks of Guideposts.

Cover and interior design by Thinkpen Design, Inc., www.thinkpendesign.com
Cover art/photo by Shutterstock
Typeset by Thinkpen Design, Inc.

Printed and bound in China
10 9 8 7 6 5 4 3 2 1

Contents

Introduction

An unknown author once said that "Grandma's heart is a patchwork of love." That love is displayed by grandmothers in many different ways, and the patchwork becomes a beautiful tapestry that colors and brightens the lives of all of her children and grandchildren.

Her heart is so big that it absorbs and heals our hurts and fears; when she reaches out in love, we gain comfort and confidence. Her wisdom may be homespun, but she's watched us grow over the years; her advice is nurturing and gives us insights we can't quite find anywhere else. Whenever we're with Grandma, we feel like our own hearts are truly home.

These *Stories to Warm a Grandma's Heart* will bless grandchildren, children, and grandparents alike. They demonstrate that grandmothers really aren't on the sidelines after all. There is the quiet power of a grandma's example and experience that indirectly leads to great accomplishments in her family. The joyful faith that draws her family back to God. The wise and knowing advice that encourages a child. These warmhearted stories will give you a wide understanding of all the different ways one can be a "great" grandmother. And if you're a grandchild, they will give you a greater appreciation of your own grandma and show you new ways to honor her.

In American Idol performer Kellie Pickler's story she sums up the commitment of a grandma's heart: "Grandma's still rooting for me, believing in me 100 percent. She's there for me. Always. My angel." Even if we only carry the memory of our own grandmothers, we feel the same—she's there for us, always.

Grandma's Bread

BY MEGAN CHERKEZIAN

ow does my big Armenian family celebrate Easter? Four generations of us come together for church and then a festive meal afterward. That's probably not that different from the way your family celebrates—except for the food. Easter is a wonderful excuse to make even more of the dishes we love to eat year round. We have shish kebab, rice pilaf, cheese *boregs* (cheese-filled dough triangles), *yalanchi* (stuffed grape leaves), and one of my favorites to ever come from my grandma Bertha's kitchen—*choreg*, a braided bread made of yeast and egg. Since it's a holiday, I get my own bag to take home. To have any choreg left over is a miracle in my family. We've even had arguments about who takes home that extra bag in Grandma's freezer.

I love it when Grandma invites me over to make choreg. She'll greet me at the door dressed as if she's going to church, in a skirt, blouse, and pearls. That's fitting because for her, cooking is a way to nourish the soul. We sit at her kitchen table, and she mixes the ingredients without measuring, flour settling in each crease in her hands. Next, we knead the dough. We let it rise, then roll it out, and braid it, each piece about the size of a dinner

1

roll. Once we fill a baking sheet, they go into the oven. Soon the kitchen is filled with the anise aroma of baking choreg.

Grandma and I spend hours in her kitchen making batches of choreg. All the while, we talk. She likes to hear what I've been doing. Then she tells me stories about her past. Sometimes they're about funny moments. Like when her kids brought in frogs from the creek behind the house. Or one of her sons decided the only thing he'd eat was cream cheese and jelly sandwiches.

Other times Grandma talks about life in her twenties. She used to dress up to go into New York City to dances. "I'd take the bus back to New Jersey late at night and run all the way home from the bus stop in my heels to make sure no one followed me," she once told me. Stylish and practical; that's Grandma.

The stories that mean the most to me are the ones that give me perspective on the choices I make. A few years back I wasn't sure where my career was headed. I confided my doubts to Grandma. "There are so many things I'd like to do," I said. "I don't know what to choose."

Grandma nodded. "I remember trying to figure out what I was meant to do. Back then there were only three job options for women: nurse, teacher, or secretary." None of those seemed to fit her, she chose the path she knew she'd love—raising her kids. It occurred to me that the wide range of opportunities I have is a huge bless, even if it makes it harder to decide which choice is right for me.

Not long ago I filled her in on my latest venture, buying home. "I'm so proud of you!" Grandma said. "I know you've been working hard." She recalled how she and Grandpa would scrimp and save for something special, especially for their kids. "One time your mom and aunt wanted a pair of Levi's," she said. "We had to put aside money for weeks, but the girls were so excited, it was worth it."

The details Grandma remembers amaze me and show me how much she appreciated, and still appreciates, every moment. A day baking choreg with her always brings me a renewed sense of clarity and joy. That's why Easter for me wouldn't be complete without Grandma's bread. Easter Sunday after dinner, I dip a piece of warm choreg into my coffee and eat it slowly. With each bite of the deliciously dense bread, I savor the stories—and the love—that have gone into making it.

Wrapped Up in Love

God gave us grandmothers because He knew
there are some things only grandmas can do.
Stories just she knows that need to be told,
Hugs that get born in a heart made of gold.
God sends us so many things from above,
Delivered by grandmothers wrapped up in love.

"In the Time of Old Age"

BY VOIGT SMITH

It had been a week since my eighth birthday, and I was still enjoying all the attention. I was savoring my last few spoonfuls of breakfast grapefruit when my father spoke sternly.

"Voigt," he said, "your great-grandma is coming to be with us tomorrow, and I want you on your best behavior."

I dropped my spoon into the bowl. "How long is she going to be with us?"

"She's not going to be visiting this time. She's going to live with us, and I want you to help her in every way you can."

I sat and stared at an empty chair. I was not looking forward to tomorrow.

The next day came, however, and so did Great-grandma. As she walked through the front door and made her way slowly along a line of kisses, I wondered how hard it would be to get used to her again. She had always complicated my life when she was around. I wasn't the overjoyed person I pretended to be as I kissed her and took her things to her room.

In my mind, three things would make our relationship difficult. First, she meant extra work. She couldn't walk, see, or hear very well; so I couldn't keep my play areas as messy as usual. In addition to having to keep toys picked up, I was given numerous chores, from making my bed to cleaning the bathroom.

Also, I didn't like introducing her to my friends. Like me, they were uncomfortable around people her age, and the introductions were embarrassing. Because Grandma couldn't hear well, her voice was always loud and coarse. This created more embarrassment when she talked about our cat. She never accepted the fact that we had named him Black Cat. She insisted on making up her own names for him.

Her physical state was what really bothered me. She seemed so different from most people that she scared me. She grunted at times, she often spent her time just looking out our front window, and she looked as if she were dead when she fell asleep in her chair.

When she had visited in the past, it had taken me a long time to get used to her. She seemed so much older now.

At first I tried to keep away from her. I was around only when it was time for the required good-night kiss. Soon, however, more pressure was added to the strain of trying to be a more loving grandson. I was appointed to take tea to Grandma, which really made me feel like a slave. She always thanked me, and so did Mom, but somehow this chore was the last straw. I did a pretty good job of holding back my feelings until one day Mom came in while I was watching TV. She was holding a tray filled with Grandma's cup and small containers of cream and sugar.

"Voigt," she said, "will you please take this to Grandma?"

I didn't answer.

"Voigt!"

"I don't feel like it!" I snapped. As she opened her mouth to reply, I exploded. With a powerful blow, I knocked the tray out of her hands and jumped to my feet in rage. "I hate taking tea to Grandma," I shouted, "and I can't stand living with her!"

Before I could finish, Mom slapped my face. My eyes started to water, and I quickly ran to my room. She gave me a chance to cool down before she came into the room. She found me sitting on my bed, looking through my baseball cards and sniffling. I looked up and noticed she was holding a black leather album and a tattered Bible.

"I thought you might like to see some of Grandma's old things." To my surprise she set them down and left the room. Curious, I opened the album. It contained pictures of everyone from Grandma's grandparents to her great-grandchildren. I was fascinated by the photographs of Grandma as a young woman. She had been pretty, as pretty as my third-grade teacher.

Finishing the album I leafed through the Bible, glancing at the passages she had underlined. Like magic, two phrases spoke to me: "Cast me not off in the time of old age" (Psalm 71:9) and "They shall still bring forth fruit in old age" (Psalm 92:14).

I read them again. Somehow those words from the Psalms broke through the rebellious barriers of my mind. They made sense to me. They gave me new confidence and patience toward Grandma. I decided to make an effort to show her more love.

Those verses stayed with me. As the days went by, I became more aware of Grandma's good points. I even asked my friends to say hello to her when they came over. Grandma would make me smile by teasing me about my crush on my teacher. I would make her laugh by telling her that she was just jealous. She started showing an interest in my car magazines, and I, in turn, showed interest in her stories about our family. Our relationship began to improve. After a while I started calling her "Super Grandma," which almost always made her smile.

I had always thought of Grandma as old and irritable. Now, however, I began thinking of her as a real person. That made my extra chores more tolerable. When I took the tea tray to where she sat in our green chair next to the front window, she would tell me about the birds and animals she saw.

Grandma kept surprising me. Sometimes I would find her paging through teen magazines. Other times I would find her praying with her hands clenched tightly together. I decided she was young in her heart and old in her ways.

A couple of years later, Grandma left for a brief visit with my uncle. I was surprised to find myself asking when she would be back; I hadn't realized that I would miss her. When the phone rang one day, I was the first to answer. I recognized Uncle Dave's voice. "Grandma died this morning," he said. His words sent chills up my spine, and I became dizzy. As I listened to his words of sympathy, I thought of Grandma and the way we had become used to each other. Her death didn't seem possible. Grandma's life had become more a part of mine than I had realized. I had learned to live with Grandma, and now I was going to have to learn to live without her.

Dear Heavenly Father,

Thank You for the treasure of the loved ones in our lives, especially grandmas. We know that Your love bridges the generation gap, and we thank you that the blessing of time spent with them makes our lives so much richer. Grandmas are truly one of Your best gifts.

Always There

BY KELLIE PICKLER

They say the best songs—especially the best country songs—come from the heart. I'm here to tell you that's true, and then some. Recently I was a contestant on TV's *American Idol*. Competing against thousands of singers, I made it to the top six before being voted off. I was grateful to have made it so far. Right away offers came in from big Nashville songwriters to write material for me. I was flattered, but in the end I figured I had to try telling my own story my own way. After all, country singing is about life. Real life. And who's going to be better at talking about my life than me?

Country songs are also about heartaches, and I've had my share of those. Most folks know by now that I had some tough times as a kid. My mom took off when I was two. My dad was in and out of jail. Neither one of them gave me much material for writing inspiring songs. That job was left to someone else—a lady named Faye Pickler, My grandmother.

I dedicated my first album, *Small Town Girl*, to her. The last song on the album, "My Angel," tells the whole story. An old dirt driveway I mention in that song ran straight from the main road to the front door of Grandma and Grandpa's house. Grandma had an easy chair that looked out the big front window, and her view went straight to the street. She could see whoever was coming from a long way off.

Grandma could see a lot of other things coming too. Like what I was heading for in life. My dad's house was right across the way, just a big field between the two, with a path running through it. After Mom took off and Dad's troubles got worse, I got to know that path pretty well. Seemed I was running toward Grandma's more often than heading home. Life was confusing back then, and I didn't ever know what to expect from one minute to the next.

By the time I started school, I was living with Grandma and Grandpa fulltime. There was a little shelf of kids' books right inside their door. My favorite was a songbook full of hymns. "Amazing Grace," "Jesus Loves Me," and all those old favorites. Grandma and I would sit together on the porch with that book in our laps and sing our way right through it. I got lost in those songs. If I was feeling sad, mixed-up, or scared before we started, by the time we were a couple bars in, my troubles took a backseat. There was a power at work in those songs that you can't put words to—that you just feel in your bones. I knew Grandma felt it too.

Grandma used those times to help me build up my confidence—something any child from a broken family can always use.

Every day when I got off the school bus, there was one person I could count on—Grandma. She was at the end of that old dirt driveway, waiting just for me. Year in and year out. No matter what. When I stepped off that bus I knew I'd see her—either looking out from the big picture window or, if the weather was warm, standing in the front yard. She was always there.

Grandma had had a rough life herself. You know the expression "dirt poor"? Well, that was my grandparents. They were teenage sweethearts. They knew from the moment they met that they were going to get married, but they weren't looking at a whole lot of options in life. Grandpa quit school real young when he got tired of being teased for wearing the same clothes every day. He couldn't even read till Grandma taught him. He got his GED thanks to her, and later on his electrical license. Grandma knew how important it was to have someone rooting for you—someone who believed in you 100 percent. And she believed in me every bit as much as she believed in Grandpa.

In all the years I knew her, Grandma's health was never good. She had rheumatoid arthritis and gout, a painful combination. She was in pain much of the time. I mean, really hurting. Not that she ever admitted it. Even if she'd been awake till four in the morning with her arthritis, she was always up the next day to get me ready for school, almost as if she drew some kind of strength from her pain.

If she was feeling well enough, she'd take me out back to pick apples or plant daffodils, our favorite flower. Daffodils,

Grandma told me, are the flower of hope. We planted bulbs all around the house. "All you have to do to know that God is up there watching out for all of us," she told me, "is look at a daffodil in bloom."

Then Grandma was diagnosed with an illness she couldn't smile her way through—lung cancer. I was fifteen and a sophomore in high school when she passed away.

After a funeral there are always tons of relatives milling around, tons of food. Then there comes a time when the last of the friends and guests have left, the last of the leftovers have been eaten, and it's time to move on. Time to get back to life—or what's left of it. For Grandpa and me, life was Grandma—end of story. Everywhere we looked in that house there was something that reminded us of her. The night of our first real supper without Grandma neither of us could sit down at the dining room table. We both just sort of stood there, staring at it. There was my chair. There was Grandpa's chair. In between was Grandma's. Empty. Like the house. Like our lives.

"Grandpa, it's too lonely in here without Grandma," I finally said. "Let's just go eat in the living room." That's what we did too—that night and the ones after it.

If I thought I knew what emptiness felt like before, I was wrong. When I came home from my first day of school after the funeral, I looked down that dirt driveway. For the first time no one was waiting for me. I loved Grandpa dearly, but Grandma looked after him just as much as she did me. Who on earth would care for us now?

It was a long time before Grandpa and I moved our meals back into the kitchen. And just as long before I could walk down that dirt driveway and feel at peace. But in time, I could. Along with everything else, it turned out Grandma had been passing along another gift to me over those years. Something I didn't know I was getting, but that was flowing into me with every song we sang on that porch—strength. The kind of strength that comes from only one place. The peaceful place I lost myself in when Grandma and I were singing those hymns. The strength of faith.

Another spring came, and one day, walking down that long dirt driveway, I could see that the daffodils were up again, bright and cheerful as ever, all around the house. Grandma's flower of hope.

A few years later, with the memory of all those porch songs in my heart, I made the long drive to Greensboro, North Carolina, to try out for *American Idol*. The rest, as they say, is history. Much as he hates to travel, Grandpa flew to L.A. to watch me perform. How much do I wish Grandma could've been there too? Well, I don't need to tell you. But, in a way—a very real way—she was. There isn't a time I open my mouth to sing I don't feel her right there beside me.

Just as sure as she sat there with me on that porch swing, Grandma's in heaven still rooting for me, believing in me 100 percent. She's there for me. Always.

Grandma's Faith

My grandma likes to play with
God, they have a kind of game.
She plants the garden full of seeds,
He sends the sun and rain.
She likes to sit and talk with God
and knows He is right there.
She prays about the whole wide world,
then leaves us in His care.

ANN JOHNSON, AGE 8

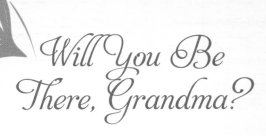

Will You Be There, Grandma?

BY SAL FATTOROSS

S alvatore, you no look nice with hair long," Grandma reproachfully told me. "I no can see your face."

Usually Grandma was smiling, but now she was scowling.

We had always been close. But as I neared my eighteenth birthday, Grandma and I weren't always seeing eye to eye.

"Grandma," I said, as I put my arm around her shoulder, "I'm going to try out for a part in a passion play. If I cut my hair, how could I play the part of Jesus?"

"You, Jesus?" Grandma smiled and hobbled away, shaking her head as if that was the most preposterous idea she'd ever heard.

To me, Grandma had always seemed incredibly old. Her stooped body nearly touched the handle of the cane that she grasped with both hands. At night, I always listened for the cane's tapping, knowing that Grandma would stop at my open bedroom door, her white hair shining in the hall light.

"*Buona notte*," (good night) she always said. And then the tapping grew fainter as she went on to her room. Often, as I lay in bed, the sound of her voice reciting the rosary lulled me to sleep.

Even though Grandma spoke little English and I knew less Italian, we could usually understand each other. I especially enjoyed her stories; many were folktales she had learned from her own great-grandmother. Mom occasionally had to translate certain words, but the suspense, humor, and love were all there in Grandma's face.

Sometimes, though, even with her family around her, Grandma felt lonely. I knew that feeling. The rest of the family seemed too busy to pay much attention to us. She was too old; I was too young. But Grandma always had time to listen to my problems, and I often listened to hers.

Now and then we talked about the Bible, God, and Jesus. Though Grandma's sight was failing, her green eyes still glowed as I held the Bible on my lap and she listened to me read familiar words of faith and assurance. Sooner or later she always said, "Salvatore, read me now about the mansions."

I would turn reluctantly to John 14:2, 3. "In My Father's house," I would read, as I'd done so many times, "are many mansions: if it were not so, I would have told you. I go to prepare a place for you."

I'd pause and take a deep breath before I could continue: "And if I go and prepare a place for you, I will come again, and receive you unto Myself; that where I am, there ye may be also."

Grandma would look at me and smile. I always tried to smile back but couldn't. Those words had simply confused me when I was younger. Now they scared me. I still hadn't made up my mind whether there really was a life after death.

Then one Sunday in January, just before Grandma objected to my long hair, Mom brought home the church bulletin.

"Okay, Sal." she said. "Here's your big chance—auditions for *The God Story* tomorrow night." *The God Story* was the Passion play that our church was planning to present on Good Friday.

When I actually got the part of Jesus, Grandma was radiant.

"Will you be there?" I asked her, knowing she wouldn't miss it for the world.

"Sure!" she said. "I be there in front row."

After that, Grandma didn't say another word about my hair and beard.

Even when I got home late from rehearsals, I always knew Grandma would be waiting up. Some nights we'd talk for hours about the Passion play, trying to imagine the suffering that Jesus endured before He rose again on Easter.

The days seemed to fly by as the family prepared for Easter. While I was at college or play rehearsals, Mom got the house shipshape. Grandma went to her own apartment to do some baking. She had insisted on keeping the apartment, even though she had moved in with us when her eyes got bad. She went there whenever she wanted to work on something special or be alone.

On the Thursday before Easter I came straight home from school. I wanted to rest before dress rehearsal.

"Mom! I'm home!" I announced as I opened the door. Then I saw Mom coming toward me. The look on her face stunned me.

"Sal," she said, "Grandma's gone. She died during the night."

I just stood there. I couldn't believe it.

Mom tried to console me. "It's what she always wanted—to die in her own home, in her own room, in her own bed."

I could barely hear Mom through the pounding of my heart. I couldn't speak through the lump in my throat that choked back my tears.

Grandma, Grandma, Grandma. My lips moved soundlessly as in prayer. *You've been preparing me all along for this. But I'm not ready, not ready at all.*

I thought of *The God Story* and how Grandma had looked forward to seeing me play the part of Jesus. "I be there in front row," she'd said. I could have gotten out of the play, but I knew Grandma wouldn't have wanted that.

Friday morning Mom and I went to Grandma's apartment. As soon as we opened the door, a familiar and comforting aroma filled the air. On the kitchen table were two loaves of bread, each neatly wrapped in a linen towel. I unwrapped one golden brown loaf and picked it up tenderly.

Suddenly an overwhelming joy swept through me. It was as if I heard Grandma say just like Jesus did, "When you break this bread, remember me." I knew—I was absolutely certain—that she was living still, in heaven.

On stage that night, I re-enacted the Last Supper. I broke Grandma's bread and thought of her. As I went through Christ's ordeal and crucifixion, my heart was breaking. I wasn't acting. I knew Jesus Himself was there suffering with me, guiding me, and comforting me.

After the play, people came up to me, embracing me, congratulating me. They said they'd been deeply moved by my portrayal of the Savior.

One little girl even wanted to touch me, insisting I really was Christ. I tried to explain that I was only playing a part, but she didn't seem to understand my words.

" *Dov'è tua madre Maria?*" she asked. I understood just enough Italian to know that she was saying, "Where is your mother Mary?"

Maria was Grandma's name. I knew the little girl meant Christ's mother, but the coincidence shook me.

"Maria is not here," I said, shaking my head.

The child pointed her finger upward and asked, "Maria up in heaven?"

"Yes," I answered. "Up in heaven. Watching from the front row."

A Better Place

In My Father's house are many mansions.... I go to prepare a place for you. And if I go and prepare a place for you, I will come again and receive you to Myself; that where I am, there you may be also.

JOHN 14:2–3 NKJV

Prepare for Crash Landing!

BY ROGER PETERSON

L ooking through the double thickness of the jet's window, all I saw was darkness. I figured we were somewhere over Michigan, but at 39,000 feet, it was impossible to tell.

I was a passenger on TWA's flight #841, homeward bound for Minneapolis. The departure from New York's Kennedy Airport had marked the last leg of my nine-day vacation in Israel where my dad, a Lutheran minister, was on sabbatical.

It had been nice taking time off from my job. This had been my first trip outside the United States—pretty exciting! It had also been awhile since I'd seen my family, after they'd moved away from our hometown in Iowa two years earlier.

We talked, laughed, and saw the sights. (My favorite spot was the garden tomb of Jesus.) On Sunday we went to church, something I hadn't done in a long time. Then we all got caught up on the latest family news. Most was good. But in one quiet conversation with my parents, I learned that Grandma Peterson had a tumor and wasn't expected to live through the summer. Grandma and I were very close. Hearing of her illness was the only sad moment of the trip. That, and saying good-bye to my parents at the airport in Tel Aviv. Watching them drive away, I felt a hurtful pang deep down inside me. It was as though our time together had reminded me of something important that had been missing in my life. But I couldn't put my finger on it.

I reached for my duffel bag on the empty seat next to me. In it was my yellow, lined legal pad. The top page was filled from top to bottom with handwritten notes—my list of things to do.

Lately my life had seemed so disorganized. Sometimes making a list helped. My eyes traveled down the page, stopping abruptly at the last item. Write Grandma.

My heart sank. What could I say? How do you write a letter to someone you love who's dying?

I stuffed the pad into my bag, turned out the overhead light, and closed my eyes.

Grandma was special. At eighty-six, my pretty grandma seemed so alive. What I loved most about her was her ability to relate to people of all ages—even kids. Once a year we visited Grandma and Grandpa at their place up near Minnesota's Canadian border. Each time we met, Grandma squeezed me till I thought I'd burst. She always said she got her strength from Jesus.

A sudden lurch in the plane's movement jolted me. Then a huge drop. My heart raced. I'd heard of turbulence, but this was different. We dropped again. My fingers clutched the armrests. A glance at the ashen faces of the couple sitting across from me confirmed my fear. Something was terribly wrong.

Suddenly, without warning, what seemed like a force of an iron hand slammed me back in my seat. The engines screamed. The plane shook violently. I thought for sure it would fall apart.

"Our Father," I prayed, "which art in Heaven..." It might do.

I couldn't tell if we were climbing or nosediving. The thrust of acceleration had pinned me to my seat. I felt the skin on my face being stretched back like putty. With all my strength I tried to move my hand, but couldn't.

"Our Father..." I kept on praying. Then suddenly the ordeal was over. The roar of the engines subsided. Our speed decreased, and I was released from its terrible grip. The plane shuddered. My own breath came out in shaky gasps. All around me people were stunned. Some were crying.

Then the pilot's voice came on over the intercom. "Let's face it," he said calmly, "we've had a small problem. But we seem to have it under control."

We would be making an emergency landing in Detroit, some twenty minutes away. Our landing gear had likely been damaged. Before attempting to land, we'd be flying low over the airport to give ground crews a look at the bottom of the jet. Flight attendants prepared us for an emergency landing. Upon impact, we would be exiting from emergency chutes.

Upon impact. The pilot's words echoed in my head. A sense of unreality washed over me as I watched the attendants hurriedly passing out pillows and blankets. Numbly I followed their instructions, loosening my tie and removing my shoes.

Flying low, we made our pass over the Detroit airport. The night seemed to be on fire with red flashing lights. In the runway area sat fire trucks, emergency vehicles, ambulances. I felt a mounting sense of dread. *Upon impact...Upon impact...*"

"Place your pillows between you and the seatback in front of you."

I tried to keep a clear head, but I couldn't. Nightmarish visions of crashing crowded my thoughts. I didn't want to get hurt. I didn't want to die!

"Clasp your hands behind your neck."

I felt so helpless. Like a baby. There was nothing I could do to stop what was happening. *Father*, I prayed silently, *why is this happening? You know I don't want to die.*

"Heads down..."

This was the moment I feared most. With our faces in our laps, we could see nothing.

"NOW!"

My head was the last to go down. It was horrible, unbearable. I sat waiting in the dark, not knowing what might happen. Waiting in the dark to die. Finally I couldn't stand it any longer. *Father*, I prayed from the bottom of my heart, *in Jesus' name, please help us!*

For a moment stillness broke through my mind's confusion. Then suddenly, unbelievably, my fear vanished and I was filled with a sense of absolute peace. The struggle was over. It was as though Jesus reached down and wrapped His arms around me and said, *"Don't worry, Roger. I love you. I'm here and I will take care of you."* I wasn't sure exactly what He had in mind—life or death—but that didn't matter. All that mattered was that through Christ I had found my peace with God.

Seconds later, I felt the impact of wheels on pavement. We hit hard, but kept on moving.

"Praise the Lord!" I said out loud.

The plane slowed then stopped. A quiet but fervent round of applause went up from the passengers. We didn't need to use the emergency exits.

The airline made arrangements for us to catch a flight to Minneapolis. I got home late the next morning. I didn't hear the full story about our flight until the TV news that night:

"Federal Aviation officials say it's a miracle that none of the eighty-seven passengers and crew were killed on TWA's flight #841 last night. On its way from New York to Minneapolis, the Boeing 727 lost control over Flint, Michigan, at 39,000 feet.

"After making two complete 360-degree barrel rolls, the plane plunged 27,000 feet in a ten-second nosedive that may have broken the sound barrier. In a last-ditch effort to pull out of the dive, Captain Harvey 'Hoot' Gibson lowered the landing gear—an unprecedented maneuver. It worked.

"Says Gibson, 'Maybe seconds before crashing.'

"Gibson then piloted the jet, with damaged right wing and battered landing gear, to a safe emergency landing at Detroit Metropolitan Airport. Six people reported bruises."

I turned off the television, dizzy with a new awareness of how close I'd come to death. I went to bed but couldn't sleep. I tried to relax by thinking of my vacation in Israel, but that seemed like a million years ago. Instead I kept reliving, in vivid detail, the terror of the flight. I kept returning to that moment when I found my peace with God.

There was no good reason why I shouldn't be dead. It was clear I'd been given a second chance. Why? Why had I been saved? I thought of my life over the past two years.

Growing up in the church, it had been easy to take my Christianity for granted. Since moving away from home, I'd just about forgotten it entirely. Maybe this was the reason my life had become so unfocused. Maybe this explained that sad feeling I had when I said good-bye to my parents in Tel Aviv.

Great racking sobs shook my body.

"Thank You, Jesus," I cried. "Thank You for giving me a second chance. Forgive me for forgetting You. Teach me how to live my life for You. Show me what to do." Finally I fell asleep.

The next morning was dark and rainy, but I woke with an optimism I hadn't felt in months. I felt alive—excited about the opportunities the day might bring. Sitting down at the kitchen table, I reached for my yellow pad to go over my list of things to do. I hadn't looked at it since the flight. Once again, my eyes went directly to the last item: Write Grandma.

This time I didn't feel so badly about the task. Feelings and ideas began welling up inside of me, aching for expression. How do you write a letter to someone you love who's dying? Suddenly I knew. I grabbed a pen. I couldn't get the words down fast enough.

"Dear Grandma," I wrote. "It's a cold and rainy Friday in Minneapolis, but I'm home and feeling pretty good. I wanted to write you because I heard that you are very ill. This is so sad and hard to believe but, Grandma, I want to tell you something..."

Then I told her about my experience on the plane—how scared I was and how I fought the idea of dying, right up until the last minute when Jesus took away my fear and gave me His peace. I told her how I knew now that God's promise of eternal life is true! Not because I read about it in the Bible, but because I'd experienced it firsthand. I told her how much more I appreciated my life. And, most importantly, how if life here on earth was good, then life in heaven would be great!

I knew I wasn't telling Grandma anything she didn't know already. Somehow, though, it seemed like the right thing to do. I figured she'd be happy to know that the faith she lived for was being carried on in her grandchildren.

I finished the letter quickly, sealed it up, and put on my raincoat. Walking back from the mailbox, it occurred to me that writing Grandma was important for another reason too. Writing Grandma was an answer to prayer.

"Show me what to do," I had prayed to Jesus the night before. He did.

Well, I've continued asking, and He's been showing me ever since.

Grandma's House

Strengthened by faith, these rafters will
Withstand the battering of the storm;
This hearth, though all the world grow chill,
Will keep us warm....
And, though these sheltering walls are thin,
May they be strong...and hold love in.

LOUIS UNTERMEYER

The Power of a Promise

BY ELIZABETH SHERRILL

My dear granddaughter,

You've been on my mind ever since this ship left New York, and I know why. You're exactly the age I was—two months short of your twentieth birthday—when Papa John and I were married fifty years ago. But it's what happened onboard this morning that's brought me down to our stateroom to write to you.

Each night, Kerlin, a schedule of the next day's events is slipped beneath our door. Lectures, concerts, dance classes, bingo games—several choices every hour. Over early-morning tea, brought to our cabin by a white-coated steward, Papa John and I go over the possibilities. Today a new one caught our eye:

11:00 A.M.: Renewal of Marriage Vows

Archdeacon Robert Willing

The Yacht Club

It sounded like the very thing for a fiftieth-anniversary celebration. So, just before 11:00 A.M. we made our way to the stern of the ship. Seven couples, all of us past middle age, took seats in the Yacht Club as a tall, bearded man with a gleaming bald head outlined the service. There'd be a Bible reading—the passage on love from First Corinthians. Then the couples would face each other and answer "I do" to the traditional promises.

"But first," the minister said, "I want us to think a bit about the state of marriage in our day." At the close of the twentieth century, he went on, the whole concept of matrimony, of a binding, lifelong commitment between two people, is under scrutiny.

Of course, Kerlin, my mind went at once to the conversation you and I had at Christmastime. I was telling you we'd chosen the *Queen Elizabeth 2* for this trip because it was on her namesake, the *Queen Elizabeth*, en route to Europe in 1947, that Papa John and I first met. "We fell in love and were married in Switzerland just four months later," I said.

And you said, "I might fall in love someday, Gran, but I'd never take a chance on marriage!"

I understood that reaction, Kerlin, with partnerships so fluid today. I remember you telling me rather wistfully, when you were in grade school, that all your friends there in Nashville had two Christmases—one with their mother, one with their father. Marriage vows like the ones we just repeated, promises to stick together "till death do us part," must seem either naive or insincere—flexible, temporary relationships appear both safer and more honest.

Reverend Robert Willing urged us old-marrieds to take a message to young people today. Can we really, I wonder? Can our experience mean anything now? So much has changed! In

1947 you traveled by ship because that was the way you got to Europe. You married because that was the way two people in love could live together. Today going by ship is an option—traditional and romantic—but you can get where you're going quicker and cheaper by air. You can get seemingly everything marriage offers quicker and cheaper too.

So why get married? What makes marriage any different from living with a significant other? Most of the weddings we've attended recently have been between couples who've lived together for years. When they take the formal step of marriage, does anything change? I think it does, and I think the change is precisely the making of promises.

Promises are scary things. To keep them means relinquishing some of our freedom; to break them means losing some of our integrity. Though we have to make them today, promises are all about tomorrow—and the only thing we know for sure about tomorrow is that we don't know anything for sure! Remember I told you how glad we were that we'd be sailing from New York at night because we'd see the lighted skyline? Well, we left in a fog so dense we couldn't even see the bow of the ship. We couldn't see any farther ahead than the partners in a marriage can.

How do you keep promises when all you can expect is the unexpected? On the *QE2* there are things we couldn't have imagined aboard the *Queen Elizabeth*. TV in our cabin; satellite phones; a small-format *New York Times* faxed to the ship each day; a Computer Learning Center where we gray-haired learners assure one another, "My grandchildren say this is easy." Change is the rule of life, not permanence.

And it's not just the outer world that changes in unforeseeable ways; it's you yourself. Every new experience—new responsibilities, new contacts—changes your perspective.

There's something that makes promises between two people still riskier: Your partner keeps changing too. In a long-ago letter to my grandmother I wrote, "On the ship today I met an Army veteran who's on his way to the University of Geneva, just like me!" The veteran, of course, was Papa John, and through the years I've kept on meeting him. Different ages, different stages—he's always someone new. I can write my granddaughter today just as I wrote my grandmother, "On the ship today I met a man." I'm still meeting John, still being surprised by him.

And of course not every surprise in a marriage is welcome. Your grandfather has written about his struggle with alcohol, so you know how difficult those times were for us. And I'm sure he never expected to be nurse, housekeeper, and sole functioning parent to three small children when I went into a clinical depression.

Yet out of both those traumas, tremendous growth and joy eventually came. And the reason, I think, lies in the power of a promise. In the service this morning the minister compared problems in marriage to storms at sea, our vows, to the ship that carries us through them. So far on this trip we've had smooth sailing, but I remember an ocean crossing when I was sure I'd never board a ship again. It was 1950 and we were returning to the States for the birth of our first child (your dad!). Ill with the pregnancy anyhow, on the pitching ship I couldn't keep down so much as a sip of water; my only relief for six long days was a moist washcloth John held to my lips.

But the ship kept going, and that's the point. John brought me that cloth. Our marriage has hit many storms. The collision of different upbringings. Financial crisis. The tensions of a two-career family (before this was common). The power of a promise is that it keeps partners together while the tough times turn into healing, closeness, and deepened love. If we drop in and out of relationships, we don't stick around long enough to allow these good things to happen.

How can I be so sure, Kerlin, that they will happen? Fifty years ago I wasn't! For the first twelve years I could see nothing positive about storms. If it hadn't been for those promises, we'd have had very few anniversaries to celebrate! Then the most unexpected thing of all happened.

It was like this trip, where we set out in the Atlantic—and now are in the Pacific! After sailing south for a week, the *QE2* entered a narrow passage carved through the mountains of Panama, emerged on the opposite side of the continent, and turned north. Something like that happened in our marriage, Kerlin. After a dozen years of struggling along in our own strength, we too changed direction.

Our personal Panama Canal was a virulent form of cancer. Your father was eight years old, the younger children five and two, when Papa John was given six months to live. In our need we took the "narrow way"—confession of Jesus as Lord of our lives—that cut through mountains of intellectual objections and put us in a different place.

A new life began for us. It wasn't just that we started to write about the new realm we had entered, though we did. And it certainly wasn't that the storms ceased; some of the biggest ones were still ahead. The new direction was not so much what we did as what we understood. Those promises we believed we'd kept "in our own strength"—I can only compare them to our sitting here in our stateroom unaware of the steel hull between us and the ocean, the engines driving the ship forward, the steersman on the bridge. It's as though we believed we were crossing the deep water by our own efforts!

God was the staying power of those promises. Marriage is His design for the fullest love between a man and a woman, and when we make those vows—even when we don't know Him—He becomes the third party to the contract, affirming our love, interweaving our lives, pointing to the washcloth by the bunk.

We can resist this grace of God, as you and I know from marriages that fail. He will not force even our own happiness on us. But every time we make a promise in line with His will, the hosts of heaven cheer!

"Do you promise," the reverend asked me this morning, "to love John? To comfort him, honor and keep him, in sickness and health, and forsaking all others, to be faithful to him as long as you both shall live?"

I was crying, as is proper at a wedding, as I listened to the questions. Crying because the answer is, "Impossible! How can any human being make such promises, when we don't know what tomorrow will bring?" But I answered "I do," because I knew I was saying it in the hearing of the One who holds tomorrow in His hand.

Don't be afraid, Kerlin, if you fall in love someday, to make that lifelong commitment. The two of you won't be setting sail alone!

With love from us both,

Gran

Example of Love

A grandmother has ears that truly listen
arms that always hold.
She has a love that's never-ending
and a heart made of purest gold.

AUTHOR UNKNOWN

The Chair That Sang

BY MELISSA YOUNG

When I was a child, my favorite day of the week was laundry day. I used to help Grandma carry the overflowing clothes baskets down the wooden stairs to our basement. While she sorted the clothes and put loads in the washer, I played house in a huge cardboard box. When the first load of wash was done, Grandma always sat me on top of the dryer. There I waited impatiently for the cold white machine to become nice and warm.

When the last load of clothes tumbled in the dryer, Grandma scooped me onto her lap, and we rocked back and forth in the old green rocking chair. Grandma told me that the chair, which groaned and creaked under our weight, was singing. To my young ears the chair seemed to send out perfect harmonies that meshed with Grandma's songs about little brown jugs and mares that ate oats. I never quite learned all the words to the songs, because I usually dozed off in her arms. When the buzzing of the dryer eventually woke me, the songs were over and Grandma was gently nudging me off her lap so she could go on to her next project.

All too soon our wonderful days in the basement were brought to a close. I went off to kindergarten, and Mom, who had been divorced soon after I was born, remarried. My new father, Mom, my two older sisters, and I moved into a house across town. Even so, I still got to spend most weekends at Grandma and Papa's house.

As I grew older, I began noticing something wrong with Grandma. She developed a tumor that doctors removed, then another that kept her in the hospital for much longer than the first one. When I visited her, she didn't seem to understand what I was saying.

Early one January morning Grandma died. Everyone told me she was better off, that she was no longer in pain and she was with God. Eventually I adjusted to her being gone, but I could never reconcile myself to the fact that God had stolen her away from me. I felt deprived—He had Grandma and I did not. Every time I came across a letter she'd written or saw a picture of her, I burst into resentful tears.

One crisp winter morning five years later, all that changed. When my alarm clock first went off, I drowsily hit the snooze button, closed my eyes, and pulled the blankets tight around my chin. As the warmth of the covers relaxed me, I drifted off...and was back in the basement on laundry day with warm arms around me.

Familiar piles of clothes, separated by colors, covered the bare gray floor. I could hear the *whir* of the dryer. I looked up, and there was Grandma's kind, smiling face. A slow rocking motion started as Grandma pulled me closer. I was a child again, nestling in that familiar lap, gently rocking back and forth on the chair that sang. I listened happily as Grandma accompanied it, tenderly crooning all my favorite melodies in the voice I had missed so dearly.

I pressed my head against her shoulder and closed my eyes, comforted by the presence I knew so well. Then a soft buzzing sounded from far away. When I opened my eyes, I was back in my bed, groping to turn off the alarm.

Suddenly, peacefully, I realized God had just reminded me that Grandma hadn't been stolen from me. In those magical minutes I had finally been made to understand that those we love will always be with us—even after death.

I looked out my window at the amber sunrise. Once again there was singing. But now it was in my own heart.

A Unique Song

You have a unique message to deliver,
a unique song to sing,
a unique act of love to bestow.
This message, this song, and this act of love
have been entrusted exclusively
to the one and only you.

JOHN POWELL, S. J.

The Spare Room

BY MARY LOUISE KITSEN

When I was a girl, our spare room was seldom empty. Granny Lyman had a knack for finding a guest for the small room off the dining room, which had a window looking onto the wraparound porch. Some of her guests stayed but a day or two. Others so long that they seemed like part of the family. Some of the visitors delighted and inspired Granny's family and friends. Others amazed them. A few dismayed them.

Dolores was one of those who gave Granny's family and friends some concern. Personally, I kind of liked Dolores and was sorry she was in our lives for only two days.

Dolores had hitchhiked into our village one rainy Sunday and taken shelter in the church. I guess we all stared at her. Usually people didn't arrive with their suitcases. Once the service ended, Granny quickly took charge of Dolores. We discovered that Dolores was a battered wife (although in those days we'd never heard the term), and she was heading for the city, where she hoped to get a job.

"You're going nowhere today," Granny told the young woman firmly. "You need some good food and a night's sleep. We'll take you into the city, tomorrow."

"You don't know a thing about her," cautioned a friend.

"She doesn't know a thing about me either," Granny replied.

Dolores showed me how to fix my hair in one of the newest fashions. And she gave me a manicure. I was twelve years old, and I'd never had one before. Turned out she once had worked as a hairdresser.

The next day Mama drove Dolores into the city. Granny went along for the ride ("and to run the show," Mama declared). Dolores didn't find a job, so Mama brought her back. The next day they went into the city again. That time Dolores didn't come back. She found a good job and a boss who was willing to give her a chance.

Annie was another short-term guest. She was fifteen and a runaway. She had tried shoplifting and been caught. Annie was given no more than a good talking to, but she felt she could never face her family or friends again. One of the local police officers spotted her and took her to Granny until her folks came for her.

"Tell them not to come for a day or two," Granny advised the officer. "Give her a chance to settle down."

After she'd won Annie's respect, Granny told her a story I hadn't heard before. "When I was thirteen," Granny said, "I stole a pin, which I'd admired, from a friend's bedside table. I don't know what came over me. I was sorry by the time I reached home and in tears by mealtime. I discovered something that day. Most everyone makes a pretty terrible mistake at one time or another.

The thing is, God forgives. And if we just ask, God helps us get going on the right road again."

Our longest resident in the spare room was Miss Ellen Judd. In her nineties and without a close relative in the world, the former schoolteacher's eyes were so bad that she had to use a huge magnifying glass to see anything. Still she read her worn Bible for hours on end. Her body was just about worn out, but her spirit, keen mind, and love of Jesus remained intact.

Miss Judd loved to play her favorite Bible game with my friends and me. We'd choose a Bible verse or story and simply give her the name of the book, chapter, and verse (or verses) in which it appeared. Miss Judd could always tell us what we had chosen. Then we would discuss it.

Miss Judd helped me with my homework—not doing it for me but showing me how. She loved listening to two shows on the radio, especially Gene Autry's Melody Ranch. One Saturday my friends and I wheeled her to the theater where a Gene Autry movie was playing. Miss Judd loved it.

Her other favorite radio program was Old Thomas. Actually it was Lowell Thomas. Miss Judd misunderstood and refused to be corrected. She liked to think of him as Old Thomas. Period.

Four years after she arrived, Miss Judd left. Not that she left our lives. She had a fall and broke her hip. A home where they could properly care for her was required. Until she died, we visited her once a month. We always played her Bible game, Miss Judd and I. I learned a lot about the Bible from that lady.

Granny's most famous "spare-roomer" was John. John was a drifter who arrived in our town and just couldn't go any farther. He was in his late fifties but looked like seventy. The doctor said that what he needed was better food and a decent living situation. Granny said he needed a home with a family for a while.

John gained his strength fairly fast but not to the point of returning to his old life. He wasn't a talker. Or a doer. He sat in the room or on the porch for hours. Not reading. Not talking. I'm not even sure he was looking at anything.

Granny invited John to church each Sunday. He always said no. Then after the service started, he'd come and stand just outside. Different members would go to the door and invite John in, but he always shook his head. Then John would return for the evening service. Granny said he must have been a churchgoing person at some point in his life.

At the first congregational meeting after John arrived in town, Granny had an idea. "We've always pitched in and cared for the church ourselves," she said. "What if we hired a janitor instead—John, for example."

There was some discussion, but finally it was decided. If John wanted to putter around keeping the church clean, the job was his. John accepted. He spent hours in the church, caring for it like a beloved treasure. But he still stood outside the door when services were held.

"Don't push him. Let him be. The Lord will push him through the door when He's ready," Granny said. So we waited.

John moved out of our spare room into a two-room apartment over a small restaurant. He still had supper with us each night, as well as Sunday dinner.

During one Sunday evening church service, the congregation was asked to select a hymn. Granny said, "Let's stand and sing 'Just As I Am.'—quickly." The pastor and everyone else looked surprised. But everyone knew Granny had that sixth sense or whatever, and so the organ started. We stood and sang, and suddenly John came walking down the aisle! He walked to the very first pew and stepped in. From that Sunday on, John always sat in the first pew.

"Bessie, how do you do it?" a friend once asked my Granny Lyman.

I remember well her answer. "I don't; He does."

Measure of Love

The important thing is not how much we accomplish, but how much love we put into our deeds every day. That is the measure of our love for God.

MOTHER TERESA

An Unmailed Postcard

BY JEANNE HILL

S omething was wrong with my five-year-old grandson. I could tell by the expression on Harrison's face the moment I saw him that windy June day in San Francisco, where my husband, Louis, and I were visiting my daughter and son-in-law. Even when I took him to the zoo, I couldn't get him to talk about it. My stomach began to churn. Never having known my own grandparents, I felt insecure about being a grandparent myself. Sometimes I overcompensated with trips, gifts, and activities.

"Sure you don't want to talk about it, dear?" I asked him again.

"Yeah."

"Well, then, how about we go see the snow tigers?"

We trudged off with his limp hand in mine. Why couldn't I reach him? *I'm failing my first semester as a grandmother*, I thought miserably.

On the trip home I tried to recall what I could about my grandparents, all of whom had died before I was born. I knew I was grasping at straws, but none of the books I had read about grandparenting seemed to help me with Harrison.

Mama's parents had died in Poland. Daddy was twenty-two years older than Mama, and his folks died before she met him. Daddy never spoke much about them except to say they were buried in Kansas. We didn't even have pictures of my grandparents; the photos had been destroyed in a fire. As a child I had felt incomplete not having grandparents.

Before long I discovered the reason I couldn't shake Harrison from his despondency—our daughter Dawn's marriage was breaking up. As soon as we could, Louis and I visited her in Texas, where she had moved with Harrison to take a teaching job. I felt the need to be a strong grandparent more than ever. But I couldn't get Harrison to go on an outing with me or even play a game.

Back home one morning during prayer, I got a strange nudge to look up Agnes, Dad's daughter by his first marriage. I had never known her well. She was in her nineties and living in a nursing home in Kansas.

The next month, Louis detoured from a business trip and drove me to see Agnes. The visit went splendidly! When I told her I wanted to visit Grandpa and Grandma Murray's graves, she gave us directions to a cemetery between the nearby towns of Dearing and Coffeyville. Then she reached into a dresser drawer and removed a packet wrapped in tissue.

"This is yours," she said gently, "because you've shown interest."

I opened the yellowed tissue and saw the faded images of a large man, seated, and a pretty woman standing by his side. It was my grandparents' wedding photo!

"There's also an old-fashioned postcard," Agnes added, "that Grandma wrote to her sister. Grandpa found it in Grandma's dresser after she died. That postcard has always been a mystery to me because Grandma addressed it and stamped it but never mailed it."

The ornate card's background of cream-colored shutters was embossed with an orange rose. "Happiness be yours" was printed in gold script across the shutters. I turned the card over and there was my grandmother's handwriting. In firm, slanted lettering she had written a short note promising a letter soon and dated the card July 1910. As slender a thread as it may have been, a warm flush of kinship flowed through me as I held the card.

"Grandma died four years later," Agnes said. "She was a wonderful woman. When people got sick or were in need, she was right there helping, cleaning and cooking.

"Grandpa was a carpenter. When the smelter went in at Dearing in the late 1800s, the people who manned it were living in tents. So the smelting company contracted with Grandpa Murray to build fifty houses. Just ask some old-timers in Dearing; they'll point 'em out to you."

The next day, at a rural Kansas cemetery, I found the graves near a big cedar tree. I knelt beside the headstone: MURRAY. SARAH 1851–1914. ZECHARIAH 1840–1923. Louis left me alone, and I started telling Grandpa and Grandma Murray how glad I was that I was to be able to learn more about them. Then I thanked God for Agnes, and I told Him how much it meant to have their picture and a keepsake.

I ended by saying, "Lord, you've brought me here. I'm hoping you can complete the circle now and help me be a grandparent to Harrison."

Louis drove back into Dearing, and just as Agnes had said, the people there pointed out Grandpa Murray's houses. They had outlasted the smelter, which was long gone.

At home the next morning, I examined the packet Agnes had given me. As I ran a finger over the postcard's embossed rose, one of the shutters popped open to reveal a verse printed in gold ink. "Many happy years be thine, full of golden hours," it went. "Both their shadow and their shine bringing forth sweet flowers."

That simple verse brought me such peace. Grandma's eyes had read it and her fingers had touched the shutters that mine were touching now. Agnes had always wondered why Grandma had never mailed the card. *Oh, Lord, could you have stayed Grandma's hand, knowing that I would one day need this message? That it's the simple things that can reach Harrison, and not the trips to the zoo, books and articles, or a frenzy of planned activities?*

On my next visit with Harrison I simply relaxed. Soon enough he wiggled into my lap and we had a nice chat. Then we watched a video together, which he had seen "a zillion times" but took pains to explain all the characters to me while I rubbed his back.

That summer, a year after the visit to the zoo, Louis and I flew Harrison to Arizona to visit us. "Grandma," he said one morning, "Mom says you used to beat the boys at marbles. Could you teach me?"

After breakfast I scratched a circle into a patch of dirt by the fence that had resisted Louis's best efforts with grass. I lowered myself to face the circle, arthritic knees creaking and complaining. But by the time I taught Harrison how to hold his shooter, my knees didn't bother me at all. The sparkle was back in my grandson's bright blue eyes.

As we played, I thought of the enriching odyssey the little fellow had sent me on. I had discovered a gentle friend in my half sister Agnes and had gone back in time to the turn of the century. I had touched a sturdy house my grandfather had built and received a postcard from Grandma Murray "mailed" to me eighty-three years before.

One day I'll tell Harrison about all this. But for now I'm just going to enjoy him—and let happiness be ours.

Simple Wisdom

Children's children are a crown to the aged,
and parents are the pride of their children....
The one who gets wisdom loves life; the one who
cherishes understanding will soon prosper.

PROVERBS 17:6; 19:8 NIV

Outrageous Okra

BY JANIE DEMPSEY WATTS

The summer I was eight years old, my mother had to be hospitalized for several months. My father worked full time and needed help caring for me, so he often sent me to stay with his mom, my grandma, on the family farm twenty-five minutes away in upstate Georgia. At seventy-four, my grandma was still vital and energetic. She tried her best to keep me busy and keep me from worrying too much. But I couldn't stop thinking about how much I missed Mama. Would she ever get better?

Grandma finally got tired of me moping around. "Come with me to the garden," she said to me one afternoon. "We're going to pick some okra for supper."

The air was so humid that my clothes stuck to me. But it didn't seem to bother Grandma. She strolled up and down the rows of plants while I trailed behind, a big silver bucket in my hand. She crouched and cut off the green prickly-haired okra pods with a sharp paring knife. Curiosity overcame my worries.

Why did she wear a bonnet, faded pink with flowers and a bow tied under her chin? "To keep my head cool," Grandma said.

"Why are you only picking the smaller ones?"

"Because the smaller ones are best," Grandma said. "The bigger ones get too tough and dried out." She dropped some pods into the bucket. "You'll have to tell your mama all you learned about okra when she's better."

Grandma bent down to pick from another plant. "You think Mama is going to be okay?" I asked.

"I don't know, Janie," Grandma replied. "But I do know our family has survived tough times before." Grandma stood and wiped her hands on her flour-sack cloth apron. She looked down at the half-full bucket. "I'd say that's a mess of okra, wouldn't you?"

"Umm..." I answered. "How much is a mess?"

"Enough to feed a mess of people!" Grandma laughed. "During the Depression we had to scrape together enough food for eight family members and the workers helping us on the farm. Now that was a mess!"

Wow, I thought. At my age, it never occurred to me that our family history was older than my eight years. I never imagined my family had struggled in the past.

I was exhausted and ready to plop down into a chair when we went back inside.

"Oh, we're not done yet," Grandma said. "We need to start cooking." She began by rinsing off each pod. Then she cut off the stems and sliced the okra. "They should look like pinwheels," Grandma said.

Juice oozed out as she cut into each pod. "They look gross and slimy," I said.

She smiled. "They'll turn out great. Just have a little faith." She scooped up a few handfuls of cornmeal and flour and tossed them on the okra. After adding a dash of salt and pepper, she handed me a spoon to stir. Then she went to the stove to heat up bacon drippings in a large cast-iron skillet. When the drippings began to sizzle, we tossed in the okra.

"Is it ready yet?" I asked.

"You have to tend to your okra. Good things take time. If you pay close attention, it'll get nicely browned and crispy. But if you try to cook it fast, it'll burn."

While the okra cooked, I asked Grandma about our family. Each story always ended with our family triumphing over misfortune: droughts, locusts, dust, tornadoes, storms, fires—even war.

"During the Civil War, your great-great-grandma stood up to a band of thieves who tried to take her favorite mare," Grandma said. "They backed down and left her mare alone."

If my family survived a war, maybe I can survive Mama's illness, I thought.

We set the table. I could smell the smoky scent rising from the okra. Grandma served me first. My mouth watered as the crispy bits sizzled against my tongue. She was right; the okra may have looked slimy before, but it tasted great now.

"Okra sure takes a lot of work," I said.

"You're worth it," Grandma said, kissing my cheek.

Mama returned home that fall. But I still visited the farm most weekends to spend time with Grandma. These days, when

I cook up a mess of okra, I think of those special moments. Grandma wasn't just tending the okra; she was also tending to my spirit. Making okra, like living life, is sometimes a struggle. But it's worth the effort if you have a little faith.

Pass It On

Dear Jesus, thank You for the ones You have placed in our lives to tend our young spirits. Thank You for the example You set of loving and blessing the children. Help me to receive Your love and then pass it on with tenderness and compassion.

My Turn

BY STEPHANIE THOMPSON

I fished my ringing cell phone out of my purse and glanced at the incoming number. *Uh-oh*, I thought.

"Stacy? Is that you?" a crackly voice asked.

"Hello, Grandma Caryle." Grandma was the only person who still called me by my childhood nickname.

"It's twelve-thirty. You're half an hour late."

"Grandma," I said, trying to keep my voice calm, "I'm at work now. We talked about this less than an hour ago. Today is Thursday, not Wednesday. I was at your house yesterday for a visit."

"Don't be silly. Today is Wednesday."

I could hear confusion in her voice. My chest clenched with anxiety. Grandma's symptoms had been getting worse lately. A lot worse. And I was her sole caretaker.

Grandma had shown the early symptoms of Alzheimer's for about a decade now—since her mid-seventies—but she hadn't really gotten worse. Just forgetful. She'd misplace her purse or lose her keys for a day or two, then find them in the laundry basket or some other unlikely place. She still dressed immaculately. She didn't slump in her chair or shuffle, as some Alzheimer's sufferers I'd seen did. But there was no doubt the disease was taking its inexorable toll. It was only a matter of time before my grandmother would no longer be able to live by herself. Then what would I do? After all, one thing was sure: When Grandma did have to move to an assisted living facility, the job of setting it up—of convincing her it was the right thing for her to do, of getting her moved out of her house—would be all mine.

"Check the newspaper, Grandma," I said now. "It's Thursday."

I heard some rustling, then Grandma was back on the line. "You're right, Stacy," she said, her voice soft with remorse. "I'm sorry to bother you at the office. But I do miss you, even if you aren't supposed to be here today."

"I miss you too, Grandma." *More than you know*, I thought as I hung up.

I tried to get my mind back onto work, but like so many times lately I just couldn't stop worrying about Grandma. Things were a complete reversal of how they had been when I was a kid. My parents divorced when I was six. Money was tight for Mom, my sister, Shelby, and me. I was shy and uncertain of myself, and Mom didn't have the time or the resources to dote on me the way she wanted to.

That was where Grandma came in. She was a colorful person. She commanded attention wherever she went. When I was with her, I felt special too. Saturdays she would take Shelby and me to the grocery store. No big deal? It was for me. Grandma made a little ritual of it, buying us sodas and then letting us cross off each item on her list till we'd gotten everything. Back then her mind was so sharp she didn't really need the list, but she knew it was something we enjoyed doing.

Best of all were the nights when Grandma invited me to her house for a sleepover. We'd make popcorn, look through old photo albums, and maybe watch a movie. Then, just before bed, we'd practice our ballroom dancing: the samba, the rumba, the cha-cha. Grandma knew them all. She'd even won dance contests. I never got much beyond the box step, but I loved watching Grandma circle the living room to the old music on her big console record player, moving so gracefully and confidently it made me feel like I didn't have a care in the world.

That was all a long time ago. Shelby and Mom lived far away. It was just Grandma Caryle and me now. The fun-loving lady whose love and attention had helped me become the person I was, slowly was losing her own personality before my eyes. It was heartbreaking—and frightening. Where was God now that Grandma, my rock, was slipping from my grasp?

Around five o'clock, getting ready to leave the office, I decided to give Grandma another call.

No answer. That was strange. I figured I had better stop by and make sure she was okay.

The evening was bitter, with a hint of coming snow in the air. Rounding the corner of Grandma's block, I caught my breath. She was standing in the middle of her lawn, wearing only her housecoat. I pulled up, jumped out, and threw my coat over her shoulders.

"Grandma!" I cried. "You're going to freeze to death. What on earth are you doing out here?"

Grandma gave me a vague look. "I don't know, Stacy. Waiting for you, I suppose," she said.

There it was again, that stab of pain, of feeling sad and frightened. *Lord, this is too much. Help me.*

It was no warmer inside the house than outside. I checked the thermostat. The air conditioner was on!

"Let's eat something warm while we're waiting for this place to heat up," I said, forcing a note of cheer into my voice.

"I must have been hungry," Grandma said, finishing the last of her tomato soup and cheese sandwich. "Is there any dessert?" One thing Alzheimer's hadn't succeeded in taking from Grandma was her sweet tooth. I found an unopened box of chocolates someone had sent at Christmas, and we dug in. I glanced at my watch. Six o'clock already. I'd been hoping to catch up on some bills tonight. But the idea of leaving Grandma alone...

"I tell you what, Grandma," I said. "Remember how much I loved sleepovers at your house when I was little?"

"Of course I do, Stacy," Grandma said, as if the idea that she wouldn't was preposterous.

"Well," I said, "maybe I can stay over tonight."

Grandma's eyes brightened. "Oh, Stacy, that would be grand!"

Grandma and I did all the things we used to. We made popcorn and looked through old photo albums—this time with me occasionally telling her who the people were, instead of the other way around. Just before bed, rooting around in the closet for a spare blanket, I noticed a golden figurine glittering from behind a stack of linen.

"Look, Grandma," I said, pulling it out. "One of your ballroom dancing trophies."

"Well, look at that," she said. "Why do you suppose it was hidden away in the closet?"

"You said you were embarrassed because it was only second place," I reminded her.

Grandma turned to me, her dark eyes shining brightly. "Oh," she said with a mischievous grin, "I'm a character!" She and I laughed like we hadn't in years, until the tears were streaming down our faces.

Grandma was still there—the vibrant, funny, strong person she always had been. The person who had helped me discover my own strength. And she always would be.

"Grandma," I said softly, "I don't want you to worry about anything anymore. I want you to be in a place where you can relax and be yourself."

"Okay, dear. Okay."

Not long after that sleepover I found Grandma an assisted-living facility for people with Alzheimer's and moved her in. It was the best thing to do for her, especially after that night I found her standing outside in the cold. The initial move was hard. But Grandma took to her new home a lot faster and a lot better than I'd expected. There's a player piano there, and on one visit I caught her singing and doing a samba to "Buffalo Girls."

That's not to say there aren't hard days. There are. Alzheimer's is always hard. What could be crueler than a disease that steals your memories? There may even come a day when my grandmother won't know me. How will I react? I'm not sure. But I think I'll be okay. Grandma's still my rock. She always will be. And now I can be hers.

My Refuge

Yet I am always with you;
you hold me by my right hand....
My flesh and my heart may fail,
but God is the strength of my heart
and my portion forever....
I have made the Sovereign Lord my refuge.

PSALM 73:23, 26, 28 NIV

The Sparkle in Her Eyes

BY BILLIE-MARIE ZAL

I used to wonder what put the eager sparkle in Grandma's eyes. Her life certainly had not been carefree. Her mother died when she was still young, and Grandma kept house for her father and the smaller children.

After she'd been married only a few years, her young husband died, leaving her with four babies of her own to raise. But Grandma believed that God "certainly knew what He was about," and without complaint she set about supporting her children with the odd jobs that she could do at home.

After her four were raised, Grandma kept loving and tending to anyone who needed her. One young girl was the talk of our small town because she was unwed and "expecting." When her little boy was born, Grandma gave a baby shower for him.

Nobody came. And so Grandma wrapped up the baby things she had bought and went to the young woman's home.

"I've come to welcome the new baby," she announced and proceeded to coo and brag about what a fine child he was. She had a special surprise for the young mother too—a dozen bright yellow roses from her garden.

Every week after that Grandma marched the girl and "their" baby off to church. Before long people were too ashamed to gossip about the sweet-faced girl. Eventually she married a fine young man.

Years later, Grandma was very ill with the flu. There was a rap at her front door. My cousin Queena had been posted there to keep the scores of visitors informed on Grandma's progress. But this time when Queena opened the door she did not recognize the handsome couple who stood there, the woman obviously fighting back tears.

Thrusting a florist's box into Queena's arms, the woman sobbed, "Give these to Mother Williams."

They left before Queena could get their names. But Grandma knew who they were just as soon as she saw the twelve beautiful yellow roses.

Grandma was poor, but she never permitted her poverty to stand in the way of helping others. One day she got to thinking about a shaggy-haired boy who passed by her house every day.

"That boy needs a haircut," she decided, The following day she called him inside, and, giving him a quarter, directed him to the local barber.

That haircut and Grandma's personal concern did wonders for the young man. He began to take an interest in his studies and finished high school with such good grades that Grandma decided he had to go to college. She had only a single dollar in cash just then, but with it she sent that boy to college.

This is how she did it. Grandma knew the president of the local college and he respected Grandma. So when a young man arrived at the school with a note from Grandma saying that she was depending on the president to let the boy stay and work his way, the president didn't have the heart to say no. Especially when he found the envelope with Grandma's neatly folded dollar bill inside.

Today that boy is a successful businessman and a leader in the community. All because, he likes to say, of a haircut, a dollar, and the sparkle in an old lady's eyes.

Once an outlaw came to Grandma's home. In those days there were still many "Oklahoma bad men," and Grandma had known him before he turned outlaw. He had a gun and told Grandma he wanted her to tend his wounds.

"Put that gun away," she ordered. After the startled man put the gun back into his holster, Grandma bound up his wounds. While she was working, she pleaded with him to give himself up, and then prayed over him. Though the man shunned Grandma's advice to surrender, he politely tipped his hat to her when he left. She was that kind of lady. Not even an outlaw could help loving and respecting Grandma.

Out under the stars in a little cemetery in Chelsea, Oklahoma, a tombstone reads, ARTHA M. WILLIAMS, BORN MAY 10, 1871. DIED MAY 2, 1943.

Grandma isn't really there. I think I know where she is now, and I think I understand about the sparkle too. I think all of Grandma's life was a journey home. Oh, she loved us, her children and grandchildren, and all the lonely strays that crossed her path. But that was because we made the journey shorter. I think she's reached her destination and sees the One her eager eyes were seeking all the while. Grandma's home now.

A Journey Home

It is God to whom and with whom we travel,
and while He is the End of our journey,
He is also at every stopping place.

ELISABETH ELLIOT

Looking for Perspective

BY JEAN BELL MOSLEY

I didn't do well on the fifth-grade vocabulary test. My downfall was the word *perspective*. Everyone else, I later learned, had such neat, dictionary-sounding answers... much more concise than mine.

It wasn't that I hadn't heard the word a lot. Dozens of times I'd heard Mama, Grandma, Dad, Grandpa, or even my older sisters say, "I've got to get out of here and get some perspective." But I never was quite sure what it was.

One day the churned milk just would not turn to butter, the kitchen stove started to smoke, and the well lost its prime. Grandma quit her chores, combed her hair neatly, put on a clean apron—the one with lace on the bottom—grabbed a bucket (her usual custom in case she found something that needed carrying home) and said, "I'm going after some perspective."

I tagged along as usual.

Across the meadow, tuned with the clear ringing notes of the bobwhites, we walked, then up the old woods road through Gold Mine Hollow. Sweetbrier was pinking every rail fence, and cowbells on distant hillsides sounded like fairy wind chimes. At last we came to a little clearing on the side of the mountain. At least it looked as if it had been cleared once and that someone had attempted to build something. There were still some old rotting poles stuck in the ground and a few overhead, as if some hunter, caught in bad weather, had constructed a lean-to.

"Did someone live here once, Grandma?" I asked.

"Yes. God did. Well, of course, He's everywhere. But right here is where I first learned that." She sat on an old split log that must have served as a seat inside what one could imagine was once a rude shelter. Then she told me all about brush arbors.

"You see," she explained. "Before the church was built down yonder," she pointed in the direction of the church a few hills and hollows away, "a preacher would come through here and the menfolk would construct these things for us to use in place of a building. There'd be fresh cut limbs laid overhead for a sort of ceiling, with open sides for air."

It all looked like a sort of grand playhouse to me. I made note of it so that my sister Lou and I could construct one closer to home.

"Right here, child," Grandma said, "is where I heard someone repeat Jesus' words, 'Come unto Me all ye who labor and are heavy laden and I will give you rest,' and I finally believed them. Believed them," she repeated, as if to underline this important aspect.

She sat awhile, as if to recapture the moment, the deeply grooved lines in her face seemed to make new and pleasing patterns. "Right here," she went on, "is where I first realized that Jesus meant everything He said, including John 3:16, 'God so loved the world that He gave His only begotten Son, that whosoever believeth in Him shall not perish, but have everlasting life.'"

There was another pause as if to let the words sink in and become as much a part of us as our beating hearts and breathing lungs.

"A visiting preacher also once said," Grandma continued, "that 'Eye hath not seen, nor ear heard, neither have entered into the heart of man, the things which God hath prepared for them that love Him.'"

The wood thrushes wove a song all around Grandma's words, as if to embroider them into some kind of woodland sampler. In the distance we could hear Jim Stacy's mowing machine. The drone of the summer insects was like music. The mountain mint smell was all around. Was there anything better than all this? A look at Grandma's face said, Yes!

I sat as still as I could, watching a hawk make his big circles high and wondering if he'd lost his way or had some well-worn, well-liked sky paths just as we did down below.

In a little while, Grandma arose to go and seemed a little hesitant about which way to start out.

"We've come after perspective, Grandma," I said, trying to be helpful.

"We sure did, didn't we, lass?" She patted me lovingly on the head. Seemed like she'd forgotten all about the milk that wouldn't turn to butter and the smoky stove.

We passed through Jim Stacy's freshly mown field, noting where Jim had carefully gone around a clump of Black-eyed Susans instead of cutting them. I took deep breaths of the perfumed air and watched the grasshoppers making long golden arcs ahead of us. We walked leisurely in our neighbor Alexander's pasture and went by the mailbox. There was a letter from Aunt Tetsie.

"Uh-huh, 'bout time," Grandma said, dropping the letter into the bucket. Letters from distant relatives were read aloud after supper, when all the family was gathered, rather than when immediately plucked from the mailbox.

Across the swinging bridge, through the paw-paw patch, up the long hill, and we were home again.

So when the vocabulary test came, I paused long and thoughtfully over the word *perspective*.

"A letter from an aunt," I wrote first, remembering that's what Grandma had put into her bucket when she'd gone after perspective. Somehow that didn't seem quite right, so I erased it. Still, I didn't want to leave it completely blank, so I wrote, "I don't really know, but the going after it is a real fine thing."

And it must have been, you know. Because, after all these years, I remember it still.

Fresh Perspective

A quiet morning with a loving God puts the events of the upcoming day into proper perspective.

JANETTE OKE

Sincerely

BY SUE MONK KIDD

Last year I sat beneath a funeral awning in the warm Georgia sun and watched as my grandmother was buried. While the minister spoke, I remembered the last time I saw her. She held my seven-year-old daughter in her lap, and as Ann moved her finger along the folds of Grandma's face, Grandma said, "Those are my wrinkles. They mean I'm getting very old."

Later Ann asked me if wrinkles hurt. But it seemed to me she was really asking about what it meant to grow old. To answer her, I pulled Margery Williams's classic, *The Velveteen Rabbit*, from the shelf and read it to her.

It's the story of a new toy rabbit that came to live in a little boy's nursery. More than anything, the Rabbit yearned to know the secret of becoming "real." One day he asked the Skin Horse, who was so old his brown coat was rubbing off, how to become real. "Real isn't how you're made," he told the Rabbit. "It's a thing that happens to you. When a child loves you for a long, long time …then you become Real."

The Rabbit then asked, "Does it hurt?"

"Sometimes," he answered. "Generally by the time you are Real, most of your hair has been loved off, and your eyes drop out

STORIES TO WARM A GRANDMA'S HEART

and you get loose in the joints and very shabby. But these things don't matter at all because once you are Real, you can't be ugly, except to people who don't understand."

When I finished reading, I said, "You see, Ann, Grandma Monk is just getting 'real.' That's all." A wonderful light filled Ann's eyes.

As the memory faded, I sat on the cemetery hill and thought about the children, grandchildren, and great- grandchildren who had sat on Grandma's lap, wearing it nearly away. I remembered all the joint-loosening miles I dragged her through the park... the afternoon I brought my baby chick into her lace-curtained parlor, poured oatmeal on the rug for him, and saw Grandma's eyes nearly pop out...the time I was learning to drive and carried her in a wild ride through the yard, narrowly missing a pine tree. More white hairs. Another wrinkle. The Skin Horse was right. It can be wearing to be loved by a child.

The service ended. Now I stood among the people beside her grave, thinking about birth and death and the journey in between. And I knew something clearly, more clearly than I'd known it before. We become authentic persons through our willingness to love and be loved—even when it means becoming worn by sacrifice, even when the demands make our faces wrinkle and our joints grow loose.

Driving away, I caught the reflection of my face in the car window. I saw the fine lines gathering around my own eyes and the hints of gray slipping into my hair. I wouldn't think of these aging signs quite the same anymore. Growing old could be a wondrous passage. And the markings of it didn't matter, except to those who didn't understand. What mattered was becoming "real." What mattered was loving and being loved for a long, long time.

Becoming Real

I see the wisdom of the world in your eyes...
Those eyes so wise, so warm, so real,
How I love the world your eyes reveal.

LESLIE BRICUSSE

She Never Stopped Praying

BY CHARLENE BALDWIN

What do I remember most about my grandmother? I think it's the click of her knitting needles as another sweater and still another story from her life took form. When I was a little girl, my father's mother came to visit us every other summer. Grandma would ride a train or bus across the nation to our Whidbey Island home north of Seattle.

She was a Scot by birth, and her visits always meant fragrant buttermilk scones rising on the griddle or a steamed pudding simmering all day on the stove. That pudding! To make it, Grandma suspended a cheesecloth full of spicy batter in a covered kettle, warning us, "If you lift the lid, you'll find out what summer's like in Florida!"

Soon after her arrival she'd hang a few cotton dresses in the closet of the room she shared with my sisters and me. She'd put folded things in the top dresser drawer, and on the dresser scarf she'd make a neat row of her pills, travel-sized toiletries and a Bible. Then, settled into a shapeless housedress and floppy slippers, the brown waves of her hair trapped by a hairnet, Grandma would invite us to watch her empty a second suitcase. Out would spill a small gift for each of us and a rainbow assortment of yarn. She divided the skeins into piles by color.

"Now this beige Red Heart was on sale for eighty-nine cents each," she'd say, patting the soft twists of blended wool in their paper jackets. "The new yarn shop at the Plaza had it at a dollar nineteen. Imagine! Who'd ever buy it at that price? So when the store marked it down to half, I got all six for two-seventy!" Chin high, eyes dancing, she'd relate the tale of her savings as if bagpipes and swirling kilts were in order.

We'd thumb through knitting magazines choosing patterns while Grandma wound a skein of yarn into a ball. Then she'd begin casting stitches onto aluminum needles, her long smooth fingers flying. That was always the special ritual, the start of the first of many sweaters she'd produce in a summer.

I remember the afternoon I wandered to the dresser and picked up the Bible, which was as much a part of her as the marvel of turning a single strand of wool into a whole garment.

"I read it every morning," she said, watching me. "That's how I start the day. And then I pray."

I considered her statement. We read the Bible and prayed at Sunday school and church. But at home, daily? This seemed no more relevant to me then than her denture cleaner and blood pressure pills.

I couldn't dismiss Grandma's comments on my growing body as easily. "Yeah," she said, cocking her netted head and examining me from head to toe with her mist-on-the-moors gray eyes. "You got your father's curls, all right. What size shoe you up to? Looks like you're gonna wear a ten, same as me."

"Just eight-and-a-half, Grandma," I muttered, sitting down cross-legged on the carpet beside her chair. Ten! It was a family curse. I hated my big feet. But I was to find out that she had a thing about her size ten feet too.

As her knitting needles clicked busily, Grandma went on to still another subject. "World War II ended in August of forty-five," she said, "right before you were born. Your dad was still in Italy, and your uncle Frank was already dead, killed in France. He risked his life to save somebody else. They sent me a medal. Gone ahead, he had, to be with your grandfather in heaven."

Grandma pulled an arm's length of yarn from the shrinking ball.

"I was at the Red Cross when the radio announced that the atomic bomb had been dropped on Japan and the war was as good as over. All the ladies was cheering and carrying on. But me, I dropped my head on the bandage I was rolling and cried like I'd never stop.

"My neighbor said, 'Lizzie, get a hold of yourself. This will mean our boys can come home now.' But my heart just broke for all the lives lost."

I wrapped my arms around my knees and rocked, absorbing her words. World War II formed the last chapter in my history book, and our family photo album featured my dad in uniform, handsome and safely returned, holding a six-week-old me.

Grandma's knitting continued until all the stitches were on one needle.

"I worked at the veterans' hospital after that, changing beds and bathing the wounded boys." She stopped to count her stitches, then looked at me, her gray eyes steely. "But I wouldn't do feet. Never. That was the one thing I said I would not do at that hospital, was feet!"

I studied the frayed spot where my big toe was poking through my canvas sneaker and nodded, identifying with her disgust for anything related to feet.

That knitting conversation happened many summers ago. Grandma has flown by jet from Florida to Seattle many times since. My husband and I drove her to the airport after her last semiannual journey. Then Grandma became too frail to travel, so my folks went to Florida to see her. I had to settle for a phone call.

"My legs won't carry me shopping anymore, honey," she complained. "My eyes don't see enough to knit anymore. I just lie here, remembering Scripture and praying for all of you."

"Oh, please don't stop, Grandma!" I answered. For I no longer dismissed daily prayer and Bible reading as irrelevant. I thought of how, one Sunday in church, my size tens had carried me to the altar of repentance in answer to her prayers, how her grandchildren and great-grandchildren were turning to the Lord in answer to her prayers, how my husband served as a pastor, and her niece worked in missions in answer to her prayers.

The thread of those prayers, like a strand of her yarn, kept on growing into garments of salvation. I hung up the phone and pictured her substantial frame, now fragile and bedridden. Then a thought came with startling clarity: Even in her weakness, Grandma presented herself daily at the feet of her Savior, feet she had always willingly washed.

Oh, Grandma, I thought, hugging the irony to my heart. *You did do feet!*

A Grandma's Prayer

Heavenly Father, please give me the ability to see things as You see them. Help me to understand the importance of eternal things, and remind me not to focus so much energy on temporal things. May I be diligent in my home, yet more faithful to nurture the most important part of my home...my family. Amen.

KIM BOYCE

A House for Katherine Red Feather

BY ROBERT YOUNG

Ten years ago, if you'd told me I'd give up the business I spent my life putting together to go build houses on Indian reservations, I'd have said you were nuts. The Seattle-based loungewear company I started with a partner was cranking out a profit. At thirty-three, I'd just married my longtime sweetheart Anita. I wanted to slow down, have a family, and savor life and the rewards of success.

Then I saw that headline.

I was in New Mexico on business and picked up a local paper called *Indian Country*. There it was on the front page, like an epitaph: "Elders Freeze to Death." How could such a thing happen here in America, the richest country in the world? I tore out the article and stuck it in my pocket.

That night in my hotel room, meetings done, I read the story again. It seemed so tragic. Somebody—the government, the tribal council—would no doubt do something to make sure it did not happen again. Still, I tucked the clipping into my briefcase instead of throwing it away. Why, I had no idea.

Two weeks later, another business trip. Another headline staring at me from the local paper: "Taos Woman Starts Adopt-a-Grandparent Program for Aging Native Americans." According to the article, thousands of elderly Native Americans on reservations across the country struggled not just to make ends meet but simply to stay alive. At the end of the piece was a phone number for people interested in volunteering. I didn't stop to think. I just picked up the phone and dialed.

Soon I was matched with a "grandparent"—Katherine Red Feather of South Dakota's Pine Ridge Reservation. I dropped her a note introducing myself.

"I am seventy-eight years old," Katherine wrote back, "and blessed with thirteen children and seven grandchildren. I am so happy to learn I now have another grandchild! Do you have a wife and children of your own? I hope so, as they are one of the most wonderful gifts the Great Spirit can give a person in this life."

I told her about Anita, and how she was indeed a godsend. Then I asked Katherine if there was anything I could send her. "Yes," she wrote. "If it's not too much trouble, I would very much appreciate a bottle of shampoo and some aspirin. Thank you for your generosity, Grandson."

Grandson... Katherine was really taking this program seriously. But shampoo? Aspirin? Why wouldn't she have such basic items? I decided to visit the reservation after my next business trip and look in on Katherine.

The letter from the Adopt-a-Grandparent program had informed me that Pine Ridge Reservation encompassed the two poorest counties in the United States. But I was not prepared for the reality of that poverty. Rutted dirt roads, dilapidated shacks, rusted-out automobiles with entire families living in them. The dwellings I passed wouldn't keep a person warm on a chill fall night like this. In the Dakota winter, temperatures sometimes plunged to sixty degrees below zero. How could people freeze to death on a reservation? The answer was right before my eyes.

Katherine's "house" was a small, busted-up trailer pushed against the body of an old school bus. The trailer door opened and a delicate-looking woman wearing slacks and a simple patterned sweater emerged.

"Grandson! Come in out of the cold."

The trailer was dark and barely big enough to turn around in, but the three people sitting by the wood stove stood when Katherine led me inside. "This is Robert," she announced, "my new grandson. Robert, these are my children. They are your family now too."

Katherine must have seen my confusion. "The Great Spirit has chosen you to be a part of my life," she told me. "We are one family in his eyes." We sat down to a simple meal of white bread and beans heated on a propane stove.

There was no running water, so Katherine needed to carry it from a well out back. It was next to an outhouse with a black flag flying overhead. "To scare away the rattlesnakes," she explained.

"They think it's a hawk." Katherine took such pains to make me feel at home that it was only at the end of my visit two days later that I could bring myself to ask her, "Isn't it hard for you to have to fetch wood and water every day?"

Katherine took my hands in hers. "I know how my life must look to you, Grandson, but all of us here live this way. I'm no different than anyone else."

I couldn't stop thinking about Katherine once I got home to Seattle. The days grew shorter and colder. I looked out the window of my cozy apartment and imagined my new grandmother in that tiny trailer, huddled over her smoky little stove.

"She needs to be in a place that will keep her warm," I told Anita one night. "A place where the wind doesn't blow through the chinks in the walls. Katherine needs a real house."

A real house. The moment those words left my lips, I knew what I had to do.

I took two weeks off and went back to Pine Ridge. Anita and a handful of friends came with me. We were going to build Katherine a house. None of us had built so much as a doghouse before, but I figured that with a simple floor plan and plenty of enthusiasm we could get the job done.

Word got around the reservation. Dozens of Katherine's neighbors and family members pitched in. Toward the end we worked around the clock, my car headlights trained on the site. Finally the last nail was driven in. Katherine's tribal chairman said a prayer of thanks, and there was a big celebration. It was the first time Katherine had all her relatives together since the Red Feather clan had been divided and made to live on two different reservations years back. She welcomed them all into her house, her eyes brimming with tears of joy.

Anita squeezed my hand, and I knew what we'd done was bigger than anything I could ever hope to achieve with my business. At last I understood what Katherine meant about all of us being one family.

Back in Seattle, I tried to concentrate on my work. Katherine would be safe and warm this winter. But what about all the neighbors who'd pitched in to build Katherine's house, only to go home to ramshackle trailers? America has about two million tribal members, and some 300,000 of them are without proper homes. What about all those people?

Building frame houses like we'd done for Katherine was impossible; it was too expensive and labor-intensive. I had to come up with a design that was warm, inexpensive, and easy to build. A little research and I came across straw bale houses. Built from blocks of straw covered with stucco, they were ideal for reservations. Straw is plentiful on the Great Plains and provides extremely effective insulation.

Getting these straw bale houses built on a large scale, though, would take organization. It required a huge investment of time and energy—time and energy I wouldn't have if I kept my day job. I sold my half of the business and started a new venture, the Red Feather Development Group, to help Native Americans get decent housing. Eventually Anita and I moved to Bozeman, Montana, in the vicinity of half a dozen reservations.

None of this would have happened if I hadn't seen those headlines ten years ago. I'd known someone would look after elders like my grandmother Katherine. I just never expected that person to be me.

Family by Choice

Choices can change our lives profoundly.
The choice to mend a broken relationship,
to say "yes" to a difficult assignment, to lay
aside some important work to play with a child,
to visit some forgotten person—these small
choices may affect many lives eternally.

GLORIA GAITHER

Sweet Ending

BY HILLARY NORDBERG GROPP

The slip of paper was in my purse, the name and address of an older woman in Titusville written on it. I'd had the address for weeks, but now that I was standing in front of her house, I was beginning to lose my nerve. Could I actually go through with this? My two boys, six-year-old Addison and three-year-old Connor, were in the car, along with my husband, Terry.

I tried to imagine how the scene would unfold. What would I say? How could I tell this stranger that I was her son's child who had been given up for adoption?

I had always known I was adopted—my parents never hid it from me—and I'd always felt special because of it. But every once in a while, I wondered what it would be like to discover that I had some distant relative's looks or that my favorite foods were the same as some great aunt's, or even that my passion for collecting dolls went back to an ancestor.

Having children of my own made me even more curious about my roots. With the support of my adoptive parents, I set out to find my birth parents. Thanks to the Internet I was able to sift through my past, accessing documents that at one time would have taken years to track down. I had a joyous reunion with my birth mother. I also learned that my birth father had died in a car accident when I was only four. What about his side of the family, what had happened to them? My birth mom wasn't sure, it had been so long ago, but she was able to give me an address.

That's how I found myself knocking on the door of this house in Titusville where my grandmother lived with her daughter. The daughter answered the door. I told her who I was, then I heard her explain to someone inside, "She says she's Jack's." I didn't have to wait long before a woman with white hair and a lined face appeared at the door—my grandmother.

"I don't want to bring any unhappiness to you," I said. "I just wanted to meet you." She hesitated then walked outside, perhaps because she didn't trust me inside. "That's my family," I said, gesturing to my husband and sons in the car. They waved. And something in Connor's smile, a sweet, tentative smile that certainly didn't come from my husband's side of the family, must have triggered something in her. Instead of being afraid of the moment, she must have sensed comfort and familiarity.

She showed us albums filled with photographs of my father dressed in costumes, playing musical instruments, and driving his prized cars that he had restored. She played with my two sons in her garden and later sent them cards for their birthdays.

I had grown up with wonderful grandparents, but she was a bonus grandmother for our entire family.

Grandmother is a bridge to a part of me that I am still discovering. I have been particularly blessed by having two families.

Perhaps the biggest surprise was her passion for collecting dolls. She had more than 200 of them displayed around her house. Talk about a link.

One thing this grandmother has given me is recipes that have been passed down through the family for generations. My favorite is the one for pound cake, not simply because it tastes good or because I've written on the recipe card the names of newfound relatives who loved it as much as my family does. It's my favorite because Grandmother taught me how to do each step. Cream the butter and sugar slowly, add the eggs one at a time, and when it bakes, test it with a knife to know when it's done.

It's what I will pass on to my grandchildren and their grandchildren. The ingredients are basic—eggs, butter, sugar—but the secret is in the baking. It has to be cooked with love.

The Light of Love

Into all our lives, in many simple, familiar, homely ways, God infuses this element of joy from the surprises of life, which unexpectedly brighten our days, and fill our eyes with light.

Henry Wadsworth Longfellow

Dawn of a New Day

BY ERIC BUZZELL

My father's family wasn't very close. Relatives were far-flung, and the standard rituals that draw a family together, like weddings and funerals, were infrequently attended. We didn't even go to church.

All of that changed when I got married and began raising children of my own. My wife, Nancy, had parents who took their faith seriously. I started wondering about God, asking myself questions like "Why am I here?" and "What do I believe?"

One morning in the predawn hours when I couldn't sleep, I sat on our back deck, gazing across the moonlit waters of the lake. "God, if You are real, let me know You," I prayed, then dozed off. I awoke to a spectacular sunrise that stretched across the horizon, filling the sky with a burst of color. In that moment I could sense God telling me He was real and the Bible was true.

I can't begin to detail all the wonderful things that happened to me after that—the pleasures of teaching Sunday school, running a church camp, and worshiping on Sunday morning with my kids. It made me realize how much faith is bound up with family. Having come to faith as a grown-up, I felt like an orphan.

I thought, *What did my ancestors believe? Did they have any kind of relationship with God?*

Oddly enough, it was the release of the Hollywood film *Titanic* that brought me some answers. During the flood of interest that followed the film, I got a call from a local magazine writer. "I'd like to talk to you about your grandmother," the woman said. "Evidently, she was a survivor of the *Titanic*."

I'd been told many times that my grandmother—my father's mother—had been on that ill-fated ocean liner. But she had since died, and I had never discussed the matter with her.

"I'm sorry," I told the writer. "I can't really help you. I didn't know my grandmother well."

"Well, I have something that might interest you." To my amazement, she explained that she had a copy of my grandmother's first-person account, written shortly after the sinking. She had tracked it down through a friend of my grandmother's.

That afternoon the writer brought me photocopied pages from the original manuscript: "My Experience of the Wreck of the RMS." Merely scanning the first few paragraphs written in my grandmother's handwriting took my breath away. This was a sixteen-year-old's eyewitness report:

> *I have a very powerful instinct, and I very clearly remember that I suddenly awoke and with a slight shiver sat bolt upright in my bunk. I sat there for quite three minutes, hearing only the deep*

breathing of my companions and the splash of the waves against the porthole, when suddenly the ship gave a violent jerk and then the engines stopped.

My grandmother, Laura Cribb, was traveling in third class with her father. They were Americans living in England, and he was a butler—a gentleman's gentleman—to the son of a wealthy railroad baron. As far as I could gather, my grandmother was going back to America with her father. She must have been thrilled, booking a ticket on the inaugural voyage of the largest ship ever built.

In third class many of the women slept separately from the men. When the ship jerked to a halt, young Laura had to find her father.

I got down from my bunk, dressed as quickly as I could, and hurried out into the main passage, which was soon full of people, all asking, "What has happened?"

I had been in the main passage a few minutes when I heard Father calling me, and I answered as loudly as I could. We went to the end of the passage to talk with some of our fellow passengers. After a while, my father turned to me and said that we should probably have to go out in the lifeboats for half an hour or more, as we had met with an accident and they would want to lessen the weight of the ship.

The innocence of this explanation moved me. Of course, the ship had struck an iceberg that ripped its side. It was sinking rapidly, but the passengers' first impression was of a minor mishap. Or perhaps Laura's father was shielding her from the truth.

I pushed my way back to my cabin, where I found my companions anxiously waiting for me to return with the news, so I told them what I had heard. Then I got up on my bunk and took down all the life belts from the racks. I took one of these for myself and gave the remainder to my companions.

We ran swiftly to the iron stairway to the second-class deck, over the gate at the top, through the salon and up to the first-class staterooms and out onto the deck.

In an emergency my great-grandfather was not constrained by any class distinctions. He was simply protecting his child.

An officer came up to us and told Father to put the life belt on me. He did at once. Then Father told me to go and get as near to the lifeboats as I could.

There is no break in the narrative here, but I felt a world of sorrow in the words that followed:

I then left him, and neither of us spoke as we expected to meet again.

They didn't even say good-bye. Laura had to wait for two boats to fill before she was able to board one.

Then, on its way down, the pulley stuck and the lifeboat started to tip. We all thought we should be overturned into the sea. Finally it was lowered to the icy waters and the passengers rowed away.

We had only been out about half an hour or so when the lights of the ship went out. Immediately after there was a most terrific,

*thunderous explosion mingled with the most terrible shrieks and
groans from the helpless and doomed passengers who were left on
the wreck of the great ship.*

Laura collapsed unconscious in the lifeboat. When she came
to several hours later, the ocean liner *Carpathia* was steaming
toward the survivors half-frozen in their lifeboats. My grandmother saw a stunning sunrise, casting pink and purple shadows
on the icebergs that floated in the blue water.

I thought of the sunrise I had seen on the morning of my
spiritual birth, a sight of enormous promise in my life. The
brilliant red sky had reflected on the glassy surface of the water.
It seemed impossible that such a simple thing could commu-
nicate so much to me, assuring me of God's presence. Perhaps
my grandmother had felt the same. "It was dawn," she wrote,
"and a more beautiful scene you could not have wished to see."
The sunrise must have been a ray of hope, reminding that her life
would go on after that terrible tragedy.

Once on the *Carpathia*, Laura was wrapped in blankets and
given a mug of coffee. A nurse rubbed her down, and she fell
asleep. When she became well enough, she found other survivors
at the notice board in the salon, searching for news of their loved
ones. It took three days to get to New York, and all the while she
believed she would see her father again, that he had been plucked
from the frigid waters by another rescue ship.

*The mood was somber. The first two days we were on board
the* Carpathia *the bandsmen were not allowed to play their*

instruments at all and were told to assist the ladies as much as possible. The third day they played hymns and other soothing selections.

Hymns like the ones I sang in church with my children.

When the *Carpathia* docked in New York, Laura learned her father was not on the list of survivors. Again my grandmother's words were not expansive, but stoic and accepting: "Such was not the case." And then, "God willed it otherwise."

That was the hardest part for me to read. I wondered if my own faith would have survived such a test. At the tender age of sixteen, my grandmother had witnessed a tragic accident in which more than 1500 people perished. She had vivid images to illustrate the terrors her father must have gone through as the ship sank. Would I have been able to trust in God's mercy if such a thing had happened to me? Or would my faith have died, consumed by bitterness?

I turned to the last page of the manuscript. On it were a few lines of poetry written in a different hand. The page had been given to Laura by her mother on the day she set sail on the *Titanic*. How prophetic were the words!

I thought of my grandmother treasuring that verse over the years. When she looked back at the tragedy of her youth, she could remind herself that God had been present. Though she had lost her father in the icy sea, she had never been out of reach of her heavenly Father.

I put down the manuscript, feeling comforted, no longer a spiritual orphan. As it had been for my grandmother, it was true for me. Even before I knew Him, I had never been beyond my Father's care.

Laura's Verse

What in the future lies
My God shall choose the best,
His loving kindness compressing,
To Him I leave the rest.
I do not know, I cannot tell
What God's love may prepare
I only cannot get
Beyond my Father's care.

Just in Time

BY FRANCES CARLETON

On the day of her funeral, I sat there very much aware of my ill-fitting dress and my unstyled hair. But my heart was at peace. I felt whole—washed clean—reborn.

The newly-widowed mother of my husband was sixty-five when she came to live with us. We welcomed her. I was in my early thirties, our children were little, and our six-room house seemed full, but not crowded.

Grandmother was a quiet, kindly woman, strong-bodied and strong-minded. We seldom crossed. We worked side by side for fourteen years, cooking, baking, and cleaning. Grandmother's whole life had been built around home and family. Sweetly, graciously, she nestled down into our hearts.

As time passed, and our children grew older—and larger—our house seemed to grow smaller and smaller. We were in the financially demanding years of educating our children and simply could not afford to build the much needed rooms.

I don't know when I began to feel so desperately tired of Grandmother's almost constant presence. I guess it happened gradually—with the crowdedness of the house and the tiredness of the years. Grandmother continued to be the same sweet, loving, helpful person, never realizing that I had changed.

My resentment grew within me until I felt as though I housed a giant of evil with which I had to constantly wrestle. I was ashamed of myself! Though I fought and warred against it day by day, it continued to dominate my life.

Almost any practical person would have said that my resentment at Grandmother's continued presence over the years was natural, that she should have found another place to live. But to ask Grandmother to move out would have been wrong. There was no place for her to go.

No. This problem could not be solved this way. The change had to come from within me. Like an impartial stranger, a part of me knew that love was the only answer. Unquestioning, accepting, understanding love could turn this unhappy situation into a happy one. I knew this and still I couldn't do it.

Then one day I fell and injured my back. A long recuperation in bed lay ahead. The next day Grandmother had a heart attack and was taken to the hospital. For many weeks I was bedridden. My husband tried to care for me and keep house between office hours and visits to the hospital to see his mother, who was in serious condition.

My days were long and lonely, pain-filled and prayer-filled. I tasted the feeling of being older and unneeded. I tasted humility. I longed to tell Grandmother what I had discovered in my loneliness. I longed to comfort her in her illness. And oh, how

I prayed! I asked God to forgive me for my past impatience and intolerance. I asked Him to hold Grandmother in His arms and enfold her with all the love I had withheld from her.

One day I rose from my pain, still uncomfortable but able to move around. I sat at the kitchen table with the sun streaming through the windows, and there I read the Bible story of Jacob in Genesis 32, contending with the wrestler. And when the wrestler cried out, "Let me go," Jacob answered, "I will not let thee go, except thou bless me!"

That night, Grandmother telephoned from her hospital room and we had a wonderful talk. We told each other how we had prayed for the other and how close we had felt to each other during the time we were laid up. We spoke of how we would try to brighten each other's days when she was able to come home.

After our talk, I marveled at the sweetness rushing through my mind and body. I knew that love had dissolved all the tension in me. That night I slept the sleep of the blessed.

The next morning we were sent the word: Grandmother had passed away, peacefully, in her sleep.

Three days later I was at Grandmother's funeral aware of my ill-fitting dress over a back brace. Physically, I was shabby and shaky from weeks of pain. But my heart was at peace. I felt whole—washed clean—reborn.

Through pain and loneliness and humility, and through prayer, I had been freed and blessed. Blessed in time to offer love to Grandmother before her life slipped away from this earth.

Blessed by Love

*Dear God, thank You for the blessing of
the love You pour into our lives, enough to
share. You help us restore broken or damaged
relationships with people we love. Thank You
for Your ways, often so unpredictable and beyond
our understanding, but always with our best
in mind, and arriving with perfect timing.*

Against All Odds

BY CHERYL DEEP

I stared at our seven-month-old baby girl, Chelsea, in the hospital crib. As I tucked in her blanket, my eyes rested on the old Dillon family Bible I kept in the crib with her. It had belonged to my grandmother, who died when I was thirteen. I cherished that Bible as I had cherished my grandmother. She always soothed my childhood hurts and fears. To this day I still miss her. The Bible had rested in her hands during her funeral service. My mother removed it just before the coffin lid was lowered, and later gave it to me.

But even Grandmother could not have soothed the hurt and fear my husband, Lance, and I now faced. Earlier that day the specialists at the University Medical Center in Tucson had finally diagnosed the baffling condition that was slowly but surely draining the life from our first child.

"Chelsea has an extremely rare birth defect called severe combined immunodeficiency syndrome," our doctor had informed us. "SCIDS interferes with the normal functioning of her immune system. She has virtually no natural defenses against infection. Her bone marrow doesn't produce the necessary cells."

I had stood statue-still and stared at him. I remembered the movie *Boy in the Plastic Bubble* about a child with the same condition. All along we'd hoped it was some obscure but curable bug causing the fever, diarrhea, and weight loss that ravaged Chelsea. I had prayed that somewhere in the mighty arsenal of modern medicine was the right drug, the magic bullet that would cure her. The immunologist carefully explained that the only option was a bone marrow transplant—a risky procedure that at best had about a 50 percent chance of success. It was our only option.

We would need to transfer her to a hospital that did this sort of operation as soon as possible, he had said. There were only a few in the entire country.

Now as I stood over Chelsea's crib I smoothed the blanket and pushed the old Bible off to the side. Its leather cover was worn soft with use. As my child slept, I closed my eyes and hoped for a miracle.

The next day we decided on Memorial Sloan-Kettering in Manhattan for the procedure because of their slightly-higher-than-average success rate. Then came the enormous problem of transporting Chelsea from Tucson to New York without exposing her to many people. Chelsea couldn't afford to catch even a cold. Any worsening in her condition would delay surgery. A simple flu bug could kill her.

Driving was out of the question. She couldn't be off her IV fluids for that long. Commercial airliners posed too much hazard of contracting a contagious disease, and big airports were even worse. We needed a private plane, but Chelsea's condition was not considered acutely critical, a criterion that had to be met before our insurance company would agree to cover the enormous cost of a jet. The catch-22 was that if Chelsea did become that critical, she would probably be too sick to have the surgery.

Lance and I were at wit's end. We didn't sleep; we barely ate. There had to be something we could do. We made countless phone calls. Finally we heard about a group called Corporate Angels, which provides free flights for sick children aboard private planes. The flights conduct normal business travel, and patients hitch along. Corporate Angels found us a flight leaving that Friday out of Denver bound nonstop for New York. A miracle was in our grasp.

"Dear God," I prayed, "now please help us get to Denver. I know You have Your ways. We'll just keep on trying."

Denver was too far to drive. We got the number of a private medivac company. But when I talked to Judy Barrie, a paramedic whose husband, Jim, piloted the medivac plane, she gave me the bad news: "The flight will cost six thousand dollars minimum," she said. We didn't have $6,000. Our finances had been stretched to the limit.

I thanked Judy and said good-bye. "Wait," she said suddenly as I was about to hang up. "I really want to help you. I'm not promising anything, but I'll talk to Jim. Maybe he can figure this out."

When I hung up I had the strangest feeling that these people would be able to do something about what was becoming an increasingly a hopeless situation.

An hour later Jim Barrie called back. "Listen, I've got a friend deadheading from Phoenix to Denver in the morning," Jim told me. (Deadheading means he was flying back an empty plane.) "If you can get to the field by six-thirty, you can hitch along."

Perfect. Chelsea could handle the drive to Phoenix. But I was almost afraid to ask the next question. "Jim, what will it cost?"

"Cost? Heck, not a thing. This guy's a friend, and he's got to get his plane up there anyway."

I was faint with relief. These total strangers had taken a huge step in saving the life of my child. I didn't know what to say. The word *thanks* didn't seem big enough.

"You could do us one little favor, though," Jim added. "Judy and I would like to meet Chelsea."

Chelsea was awake and even a bit playful when Jim and Judy arrived at the hospital. While Jim talked to Lance about finding our way around the Phoenix airport, Judy and I chatted. Her eyes kept flitting over to the crib. Then I noticed she was staring at Grandma's Bible. One time when Judy was leaning over Chelsea, her fingers brushed against it. Finally, as they were about to go, Judy asked, "Where are you from?" I told her Pittsburgh.

"I'm from Pittsburgh too," she said slowly. "Well, Carnegie actually."

"My mother is from Carnegie," I said. I felt a shiver go through me. "Virginia Everett. Dillon was her maiden name."

"Virginia Dillon?" Judy said, eyes wide. "My father was Howard Dillon."

"Uncle Howard?" I was stunned.

Judy nodded. It was as if a current of electricity had jumped between us. Now I could see why her face had seemed faintly familiar. Judy Barrie was my cousin Judy Dillon. "I haven't seen you since..." I started to say. Judy's eyes jumped again to the Bible.

"Since Grandma's funeral twenty years ago," she finished the sentence. "That's the Bible she was holding."

We fell into each other's arms. I knew then that all would be well with Chelsea. The odds against this crossing of paths were simply too great. This was meant to be.

Chelsea got her bone marrow transplant and four months later she left the hospital with a healthy immune system. She is, as they say, a medical miracle.

Then there was that other miracle. I like to think of it as my grandmother's miracle. In a sense, even twenty years after her funeral, she was reaching out to comfort me and to assure me that with God all things are possible.

Grandma's Miracle

In the presence of hope—
faith is born.
In the presence of faith,
love becomes a possibility!
In the presence of love—
miracles happen!

DR. ROBERT SCHULLER

Grandma Hita

BY CYNTHIA BROOKS

When I was nine years old the thought of death petrified me. I could not stand the prospect of anyone close to me being taken away, nor could I face the eternal emptiness that I feared was death. *Dead*. The very word sent me into panic.

One evening, about a year after the birth of my sister, my father announced that my mom's mother, Grandma Hita, was moving in with us. (I called her Grandma Hita because she always called me *mi jita*—her shortened version of *mi hijita*—"my little child" in Spanish.) Dad explained that because of Grandma's failing health she would not live alone much longer.

My heart raced and I felt dizzy. Grandma Hita was old and might die while she was with us!

But after Grandma moved into the baby's room, everything seemed to be all right. Grandma's presence calmed us all. She shuffled quietly throughout the house and was glad to do laundry, iron shirts, start dinner, and mend clothes. Every night she sat on the edge of her bed and changed the bandages on her badly ulcerated leg sores.

"How did you get those sores, Grandma?" I asked one night. In her broken English she told me that she had been pregnant most of her childbearing years—twenty-one times! Even though only six of her children had survived, the pregnancies had been hard on her body, and her legs in particular. But she never complained.

I often wandered into Grandma's room and talked with her as she mended a blouse or wrote a birthday card to one of her other grandchildren. I loved to lie on her bed and visit with her. She became my closest confidante, and I went to her with many of my problems.

One Saturday morning my mother left me a long list of chores. I was not allowed to go out and play until every job was crossed off the list.

"How am I going to do all of this?" I whined.

Grandma Hita spoke softly, "I help you, and little by little, mi jita, we get it all done."

I noticed Grandma's lips moving while we worked. "What are you doing, Grandma?" I asked.

"I pray to the Lord, mi jita," she said. "God will help us do our work."

Another day I came running home in tears. I was eleven. Kathy, a neighborhood girl, had just told me the family I regularly babysat for had asked her to babysit the next Saturday night. I cried in Grandma's lap as I questioned why the family I loved so much would drop me so abruptly. I had tried hard to be the best babysitter ever, bathing the three little boys and reading them bedtime stories. I had thought I was appreciated, but now my heart was broken.

Grandma brushed my hair away from my face and whispered, "Don't worry, mi jita, justice wins out in the end. Jesus knows what is in your heart. He take care of everything." But I had a hard time believing her.

The next morning, Dale, the mother of the boys, called and asked me to come over. I walked the block to her house petulant and hurt. Was she going to tell me Kathy would become their regular babysitter?

When we sat down, Dale placed a pearl ring in my hand. "This belonged to my mother. Since I have no daughters, I want you to have it. You have become such a part of our family that we want you to know how much we love you."

She invited me to attend the mother-daughter banquet with her at her church on Saturday night. So that's why she had asked Kathy to babysit! Grandma had been right again.

As the days turned into years, Grandma became an integral part of our family and insisted on helping in every way possible. She mended my sister Helen's cheerleading skirt and stitched my brother Kenny's pants. My baby sister, Mary Anne, often took her nap in Grandma's arms.

One evening as I sat on the edge of her bed, I choked out, "Grandma, I don't ever want you to die."

Instead of recoiling in horror, she laughed out loud. "Oh, mi jita, you don't mean that. I am so tired. I looking forward to no more sore legs. I looking forward to seeing Jesus and resting in his arms."

"But I'll miss you so much!" I cried.

"Oh, no, mi jita, I'm never going to leave you." I looked into her eyes and could not believe what I saw. She was so old and close to death and yet she was happy to talk about it. She held me tight and continued to chuckle.

I watched Grandma closely and noticed how often she prayed. Not just at church or before bed but almost constantly. I too prayed for the serenity Grandma felt about death.

Shortly before the weekend of my aunt and uncle's twenty-fifth wedding anniversary, Grandma went to stay with them to help prepare for the festivities. Mom, Dad, Mary Anne, and I traveled to the church on Saturday morning for the anniversary Mass. We waited excitedly until my aunt and uncle finally appeared and walked down the aisle to the wedding march. But as they neared our pew I could see my aunt's face was puffy from crying. As she approached she leaned over to my mother and said, "Mama's just had a stroke. She's in the hospital."

I barely remember the next two days except for the constant comings and goings. I wasn't allowed to visit the hospital— Grandma wasn't conscious, I was told—and I kept myself busy trying to entertain four-year-old Mary Anne.

A few days later I woke to see my dad sitting on my bed. "Grandma died just a little while ago," he whispered.

I hugged my dad, and as I did, instead of being engulfed by the fear and panic I had always expected and dreaded, I felt a surprising peace and calm. Death had happened. My grandmother, whom I loved intensely, had died. But I knew she was where she wanted to be. That night I slept better than I ever had.

I am grown now and have a child of my own. At times I still long to lie on Grandma Hita's lap. I miss her. But when my daughter is overwhelmed by a pile of homework, I tell her "Little by little, mi jita." Or when my husband laments some injustice at his workplace, I say, "Don't worry, Honey, justice wins out in the end. Jesus knows what's in your heart." I feel again the gentle peace I knew when I nestled in Grandma Hita's lap. And I smile, knowing Grandma is indeed watching over me—and we are both resting where we belong.

What Matters

This era will pass so quickly, and the present stresses will seem insignificant and remote. What will matter to you at the end of life will be the loving relationships you built with your family and your readiness to meet the Lord.

JAMES DOBSON

"Hey, Doodle!"

BY B. J. CONNOR

When our daughter Nichole was just eleven days old, Mike and I made one of our many relocations, this time from South Dakota to Durham, North Carolina. I had prayed our next move would land us near my parents in Pennsylvania. I had loved living near my grandmother, and being near grandparents was something I wanted for Nikki. Now she would be missing something precious.

We had been settled in our little white frame house in Durham for only a day when I heard a knock on the door. Outside stood an elderly woman wearing silver-rimmed glasses that matched her permed hair. Her face was creased with apple-doll wrinkles. She seemed pleasant enough to be a grandma, but she was so different from Nikki's younger, active real grandmom.

"Hey!" the slightly stooped woman said, smiling. She handed me a chocolate cream pie and a bouquet of roses. "I'm Sudie Cole. My husband, Marvin, and I live behind you. I can't stay long because I have to get back to Marvin—he's got arthritis real bad—but I wanted to welcome y'all. Did I hear you just had a baby?"

I took her to our bedroom, where Nikki was napping. Sudie said admiringly, "Well, isn't she something! Marvin and I never had children. You'll have to bring her over to see him."

A few days later, with time hanging heavy in a town where I hardly knew anyone, I hoisted Nikki in her carrier up the Coles' front steps.

"Hey!" Sudie exclaimed, which I now understood meant hello. "Marvin, look who's come to see us. Hey, Doodle!" She greeted Nikki warmly.

We entered the small, immaculate front room, and I took in the scene—antique velvet maroon sofa and chairs, marble-topped tables, television, fireplace, and desk. It was very formal—the exact opposite of my parents' make-yourself-at-home living room. I sat stiffly on the unyielding Victorian sofa. Marvin sat with a card table in front of him, his walker beside him. Short, bald, and twisted from arthritis, he looked like a gnome with his sharp nose and gnarled fingers. In contrast to my dad's blue work shirts and jeans, he wore a crisp, striped dress shirt, and brown dress pants.

"Let me see this little girl," Marvin said eagerly.

I set Nikki's infant seat on the card table facing Marvin. "Hey, Princess," he said, marveling at her face, touching her dainty fingers with his curved arthritic ones. She tilted her head and gave him the flicker of a smile.

Sudie prattled on about how she had taught elementary school for forty years and how Marvin had worked in a factory. Marvin pointed to the clocks on the mantel and desk and told me he had restored them.

"G'bye, Princess," he said to Nikki when I indicated we had to go. "Y'all come back and see the Coles."

Sometime, I thought. How I missed Nikki's grandparents.

Mike was gone long hours at grad school and his part-time job. During the day our street was like a ghost town, with younger neighbors at work. I found myself visiting the Coles every few days.

"Hey, Doodle!" Sudie would always say, welcoming and nuzzling her cheek. Once company stopped by while I was there. They asked the Coles, "Is this the baby y'all talk about all the time?" Sudie and Marvin nodded proudly.

Soon Nikki was too big and active for the card table, so she crawled on the Coles' carpet and climbed onto their sofa. She took her first steps in front of their TV.

Two years after our move I set aside an afternoon to bring our photo album up to date. As I sorted through pictures, I marveled at how many there were of the Coles. Finally I placed my selections in the album then started writing captions. About the second or third time I had written "Nikki's 'Durham grandparents,'" I paused. I had fretted and stewed when we had ended up far away from Nikki's grandparents. Now I realized we had landed right next door to as fine a set of grandparents as I could have hoped for. "Dear Lord," I prayed, "Thank you for the Coles—and for answering my prayer for Nikki so beautifully."

When the Coles moved to a retirement home nearby, three-year-old Nikki became a mascot, scampering among the residents. She helped push Marvin's wheelchair, and she entertained us by singing into Sudie's wooden cane as if it were a microphone. When people asked Sudie, "Is that your granddaughter?" Sudie answered proudly, "She's no kin to us, but we claim her."

When Nikki was three and a half, I gave birth to our son. I called the Coles from the hospital minutes after Sean was delivered, leaving Mike to call Nikki's "real" grandparents.

"Guess what I'm holding in my arms!" I teased Sudie ecstatically.

"Not a baby!"

"If it's not, I don't know what is!"

Two months later in May, we planned a visit to the Coles. It was bittersweet because we were about to move for Mike's new job. After church we loaded the children into the car. I ran back to the refrigerator for a special box I had picked out at a florist's—a corsage for Sudie. Because that's what you give a grandma on Mother's Day.

Special Grandparents

Grandparents of all kinds are special,
they are friends of treasured worth.
And one who knows their love
has the greatest gift on earth.

AUTHOR UNKNOWN

Grandparents 101

BY RACHEL KOVACINY

Easter break. Time to ditch the books and hit the beach, right? Except I was in an assisted-living center, suitcase in hand, looking for my grandparents' apartment. I passed the lounge and looked in. White-haired men and women playing cards. Scrabble. A TV going in the background. No one under fifty in sight, and I was going to spend five whole days here.

How had I gotten myself into this? Well, reason number one was my sociology research paper. I had a ton of reading. That's what the books in my suitcase felt like. Reason two: As my parents not-so-subtly reminded me, "Your grandparents are in their eighties. They won't be around forever." Translation: Spend some time with Grandma and Grandpa. Reason number three: Larry. The spring dance was coming up, and he'd asked me to go with him even though we'd never gone on a real date. Were we just good friends or, as I secretly hoped, something more? Sometimes I had trouble getting my mind off him. Was I even old enough to know what love was? Could I trust my feelings? Maybe this time away would give me a chance to sort things out.

There was my grandparents' place. I knocked, and the door opened quickly.

"Look who's here!" Grandpa ushered me into their apartment. Grandma practically leapt out of her rocking chair to give me a hug.

They were so happy to see me I felt guilty about having misgivings. *God, I know a retirement community doesn't have much to offer a nineteen-year-old, but I don't want to hurt Grandma and Grandpa's feelings. Please keep me from getting too bored. I want to make something positive out of this week.*

I barely stashed my suitcase before they whisked me to the main dining room for lunch. "This is our granddaughter Rachel," Grandma announced proudly.

Boy, did everyone fuss over me. They wanted to know what classes I was taking and what my roommates were like. "You have such beautiful long hair," one woman told me. She turned to her husband. "Remember when I used to wear my hair long?" He kissed her cheek.

Pretty sweet.

After lunch, it was off to the lounge to play games and hang out. "Come join my friends for some Scrabble," Grandma said.

"Sure." It would be a harmless way to pass an hour. In the end, a ferocious battle waged all afternoon. Those grannies beat me good. I guess I should have realized that whatever I'd picked up in class would be no match for the vocabulary they'd acquired over eight decades. These ladies were sharp.

Which reminded me—I had all that reading to do. I tried to slip away after dinner, but Grandpa steered me back to the lounge. "Why would they call it a break if you weren't supposed to take one?" His friends were waiting by the pool table, a cue stick chalked for me.

How could I say no to such chivalry? It was all a front. Grandpa and his buddies didn't show me any mercy. They sank shot after shot.

"Eight ball, corner pocket," Grandpa said confidently. *Clunk!* He let out a whoop.

Grandma came over. "John, Rachel is our guest," she said in mock disapproval. "Surely she deserves better treatment."

I giggled. The two of them exchanged glances and burst out laughing too.

Grandpa took Grandma's hand and didn't let go the whole way back to their apartment. That was really sweet.

Thanks, God, for a good first day here. Only four more to go.

They didn't just go. They flew. Life at the center wasn't that different from college. Hanging out with friends. Ongoing Scrabble tournaments. Lots of girl talk.

My last afternoon, one of Grandma's friends asked, "Do you have a boyfriend?"

"Sort of," I said. "This guy, Larry, asked me to the spring dance."

"Do you think you two will get married?" The question took me aback. "Well, I haven't really known him that long. We're not even officially dating. But I have a feeling about him. I can't explain it..."

"I met my late husband in fifth grade," she told me. "We were just friends then, but I knew he was the one for me. When you know, you know. You'll feel it right here." She touched her chest.

I smiled and changed the subject, but it was hard not to think about Larry. Everywhere I turned, I saw the kind of love that I hoped to find yet hadn't been sure existed. Love that, with each passing year, makes a woman more beautiful in her husband's eyes. That grows with a couple and keeps them walking through life together, holding hands, like Grandma and Grandpa. It was all around me, as if God were trying to show me what love was all about.

Too soon I was hugging my grandparents good-bye. "Rachel, we're so glad you spent your Easter break here," Grandma said.

"Sorry you didn't get your reading done," Grandpa added with a wink.

"I'm glad too," I said. "I learned way more than I could have from my books."

Maybe you can guess the end of my story. I went to the dance with Larry that year, and two years later, I married him. As Grandma's friend said, "When you know, you know. You'll feel it right here."

Sweetness of Love

Love is something like the clouds that
were in the sky before the sun came out.
You cannot touch the clouds, you know;
but you feel the rain and know how glad the flowers
and the thirsty earth are to have it after a hot day.
You cannot touch love either; but you
feel the sweetness that it pours into everything.

ANNIE SULLIVAN

Take Another Look

BY JAMES STANLEY JENNINGS

S trange how quickly the direction of a life can change. At seventeen, I had graduated from high school and was talking about going to college when I got into a mess that had no bottom. I just kept sinking lower and lower. I would still be sinking, I guess, if it weren't for something that happened to me a few months ago—right here in prison where I'm writing this.

My childhood was marred by a broken home, but I was lucky. My grandparents picked up the pieces and gave me such a wonderful home that I never really missed my real mother and father. They drifted out of the picture, and my grandparents more than filled the void. I realize now how much it must have hurt them when I went out on my own at age eight and then was sent to prison for passing bad checks at twenty.

For the next seven years I was in and out of jail. Last fall I was given another sentence for passing bad checks, and it wouldn't have been any different from the other raps except for a strange letter I received—a letter from Grandpa.

Grandma had written often, and she kept encouraging me to get straightened around. "God wants you to find a purpose in this life, Stanley. He's ready to forgive and wipe the slate

114

clean," she once wrote. But now came an envelope addressed in Grandpa's handwriting.

I tore it open, but it seemed to be empty. Shaking it, a picture of a young boy dropped out. A picture of me. On the back were written these words: "Stanley Jennings—aged six—he was such a good boy. I wonder what happened to him. Grandfather."

For a long time I stared at those words in a kind of fog. Often I had been lectured and scolded, but this—this was somehow different. The words went through me like a sword. *What had happened to me?* Tears began to trickle down my cheeks.

Grandpa's question haunted me day and night. Whenever I thought of the picture I asked, "What did happen?" I tried to rethink my childhood—isolate some reason for my predicament. I couldn't come up with an answer. However, little vignettes of the past played on my mind, especially at night.

I remembered when I was eleven and had bought some baby chicks. I'd ordered fourteen hens and one rooster and put them in a backyard pen. The next morning one of them was dead, trampled to death. I was heartbroken. Grandpa came by and saw me crying. When he investigated, he told me the trouble. I had bought fourteen roosters and one hen.

"Stanley," he said, "the hen should have been separated. She couldn't exist in such an unbalanced situation. It's the same with people—they need support from their own kind."

In a way, my life had been much like that hen's. When I cut myself loose from the security and stability of my grandparents,

I entered a world I was unprepared for. The values they had tried to implant in me were valueless to the people with whom I came in contact and, like the hen, I folded. Not a physical death, but a living death.

How do I get off this track? I asked myself. The answer seemed to lie in the faith which sustained my grandparents. I began to think about God again...about some of the things the Bible said of Him. I found myself saying a prayer. It had been years since I had uttered His name—in prayer anyway.

It was past midnight. All the world seemed quiet, as though someone was waiting with reverence for me to break the silence. Then I heard myself say, "Dear God, please help me...I can't do it alone."

In the following days I felt different—I really felt changed. Somehow the years of tension vanished and I was more at ease than I'd ever remembered. That Sunday I went to the prison chapel and have done so every Sunday since. I met others who also were searching for God behind those tall gray walls.

A young prisoner who had, among other things, stolen a Bible, came to me one day and said, "Stan, I've been watching you lately and you've changed. Do you think I could change? I've tried everything; maybe God is the answer for me too."

"You can change with His help," I answered, trying very hard to hide the emotion rising within me. This boy who had stolen a Bible also had stolen God's love along with it.

"But how do I begin?" he asked.

I hesitated. I felt my answer was important, and I didn't want to make a mistake. Then I remembered my own miracle. My answer came easily. "First of all, get a picture of yourself when you were a little boy, then take a look at yourself in a mirror. God will do the rest."

Sustaining Faith

He who began a good work in you will carry it on to completion until the day of Christ Jesus.

PHILIPPIANS 1:6 NIV

The Adoption of a Grandma

BY PATRICIA A. LORENZ

I t'll be great!" I said as much to myself as to my husband and four children. "Just like having a real grandma! We'll have her over for Sunday dinners. Introduce her to our friends. She never had any children of her own. Imagine how lonely she must be!"

As I finished tossing the salad for supper, my mind was on the Adopt-a-Grandparent program sponsored by our church. It sounded like such a marvelous idea for our family. Our children's grandparents lived far away in other states, and I felt we definitely needed a hometown grandma.

I could already smell spicy gingerbread cookies baking in her oven. I imagined sitting in her living room in an old cane rocker listening to stories about her girlhood days.

Visions of turning her life around for the better danced before my eyes. I would fix a little extra food once or twice a week and provide her with some good home-cooked meals. And that knitted shawl that had belonged to my mother...wouldn't it be just the thing for our new grandma?

I told my husband, "Think of the advantages the children are going to receive! They'll learn to care about older people and to make time for them. They'll learn all about the olden days. Maybe she'll teach them how to bake those wonderful German pastries. The director told me her name is Sarah. She was born in Germany in 1890!"

"But, Pat..." my husband started to object.

"And she can teach the girls how to crochet. I'm sure she does that sort of thing. All grandmas do!"

The day finally arrived when we were to meet Grandma Sarah. She lived by herself in an apartment complex for the elderly.

The six of us—four children, my husband and I—all crowded into her tiny living room. Hats, coats, scarves, and gloves were piled in a mountainous heap on one chair in her closet-sized kitchen.

I spoke first. "Sarah, we're so glad to have you for our grandmother. Would you like to come to our house for dinner next Sunday? And it you need to do any shopping, I'll be glad to take you this week." I was blubbering with enthusiasm, hoping it would rub off on the rest of my family.

Sarah pushed back a stray curl of white hair and tried to tuck it into the neat twist on the top of her head. She spoke slowly, precisely. "My dear, I broke my hip last winter, and I don't go out in the cold anymore. I'm afraid I might fall again. But I don't mind. It's not important to me to get out."

"Oh, goodness," was all I could mutter. "But what about church? Can't we at least take you to church with us?" I was determined to get her on our social calendar.

"No, not even that. Never missed a Sunday for nearly ninety years, but since last winter I don't even go to church anymore. Two nice folks from the visitation committee bring me communion every Sunday. So I don't mind not going. And I watch services on TV."

"Well then, we'll just have to figure out something else to do together. How about games? Do you play Monopoly or checkers? I noticed the lounge area down the hall with the game tables."

"My eyes, they just aren't what they used to be. Can't read the newspaper anymore. I listen to the radio a lot though. The big-print magazines are fine. But games? No. Just can't see well enough. I'm ninety-three, you know!"

Sarah was starting to get to me. The more enthusiastic I was about trying to make her life happier and more fulfilling, the more she seemed to cut me off at every pass.

"Well, we'll just visit you then, and talk!" Out of the corner of my eye I saw my teenage daughter counting the tiles on the ceiling. My other daughter was fidgeting with the buttons on her sweater.

I continued, "The girls can come over after school some days. Maybe you can teach them to knit or crochet?"

Before Sarah could answer, I hurried on. "And Michael likes to walk to the shopping center next to your apartment with his best friend. They can stop in to see you every Saturday. You know how boys like cookies and milk from Grandma!"

Sarah pulled a bright orange, brown, and gold afghan over her knees. She eyed Michael, who was writing his name on the steamy living room window with his finger. "Well, I do get lots of company. My sister comes every week. And my niece. I have the nicest niece. Reminds me of you, my dear. About your age too. Five kids though. Her oldest just got married. Here, I'll show you the pictures."

At that moment, Andrew, our three-year-old, announced that he wanted a drink. He ran after Sarah, who was searching for the wedding pictures. Before I could grab him he'd knocked a plant off the coffee table. My husband shot me one of those "It's time to get out of here" looks. I cleaned up the potted plant mess then hustled the children into the kitchen for their coats.

"I'll come back to visit you this week, Sarah. Andrew's getting tired. That's why he's acting up."

"Well, I wouldn't know. Never had any children of my own. Just watched my nieces and nephews grow up from a distance. Haven't had any experience as a grandma. The church folks must have felt that I needed this program. Actually, I'm not a bit lonely. And I sure don't know a thing about being a grandma."

"You're doing great. It'll all work out," I muttered while I fiddled with Andrew's jacket. "Oh, I almost forgot. We brought you some presents. A canned ham, a candle, and this shawl that belonged to my mother."

Sarah looked at the gifts and responded curtly. "My, what will I ever do with that much ham! It'll go to waste. I get meals from Meals on Wheels. They bring my food every noon with plenty left over for supper. I'm not supposed to use my stove. Everyone's afraid I'll burn the place down, I guess."

She chuckled for the first time, then went on. "But you know, I don't miss it. Baking schmaking. Who needs all that work? Now I relax. You take the ham home. Your big family needs it. And the shawl too. Dear, I have a drawerfull of shawls. And the candle. It's lovely, but please, take it. I give most of my things away. Too much work dusting and cleaning everything. When you're ninety-three you'll want life simple too."

On the way home hot tears rolled down my cheeks. "How could she be so heartless! She wouldn't even accept our gifts!"

My husband touched my arm and said slowly, "Honey, you're expecting too much. She doesn't seem to be sad or lonely. And certainly not helpless. She's content with her life the way it is. Why should we clutter it up? You just can't rush in and start changing her life."

"Changing her life? This grandparent program is a wonderful opportunity for her! She needs us!" Later, musing about the situation, I recalled the verse our church had used when they started the Adopt-a-Grandparent program. "Rise in the presence of the aged, show respect for the elderly" (Leviticus 19:32 NIV). Not only did Sarah need us, but it was my duty to show my respect for her as best I could.

Three days later, my spirits and optimism renewed, I popped in on Grandma Sarah. Six nuns, all dressed in short black dresses and veils, were also there to greet me.

Sarah explained. "My one sister, she's a nun you see, and these are her friends. They visit me every week."

I stopped over once again the next Saturday. This time I interrupted a visit by Sarah's niece and her son. They were just sitting down to an impromptu lunch of cold cuts and deli salads that her niece had brought.

Sarah was cordial enough. When she introduced me to her niece she said, "This is the lady whose family adopted me as their grandma. Imagine, me, a grandma!"

Sarah tried to find room for me at the tiny kitchen table. I told her I'd already eaten and that I'd wait in the living room. As I turned around she handed me a box of pictures. "Here, look at these. It's the Christmas party the landlord had for all of us here at the apartment," she said. "We have a party every month."

I settled into the overstuffed sofa, let the afghan fall around my shoulders, and basked in the warmth of the room. I fumbled through the pictures. In every one Sarah was surrounded by laughing, happy people. I gazed at these pictures of happiness and listened to the bright chatter between Sarah and her niece.

Was this a sad, lonely old woman? Indeed not. My husband had been right all along. Sarah's life was already filled with love, with people, with small adventures and happy memories. Incredibly alert and healthy for her age, she was enjoying the last years of her life. What right did I have to interfere?

I had even been taking away some of her rights. She had a right to her privacy, a right to choose her own friends, a right to be alone when she wanted, and a right to continue depending upon those with whom she felt most comfortable.

The verse from Leviticus came back to me: "Rise in the presence of the aged, show respect for the elderly."

Now I knew I wasn't showing Sarah respect at all. I was not respecting what she wanted. At last I began to understand that it was I who was in need. I had been willing to include her in some of my family activities with the hope of receiving so much more. I'd expected monumental gifts from Sarah—her precious time, her talents, the wisdom of her years, her influence upon my children, and the tales of her past. I wanted her love, her devotion, and her gratitude.

It was time to go. Gently I refolded the warm afghan and placed it on the back of the sofa. I knew I'd never say good-bye to Sarah for good, but when I gave her a hug that day I knew it was the beginning of a much gentler, less frequent, less demanding relationship. Sarah had earned her peaceful, contented lifestyle, and I would never play havoc with that again.

A Happy Life

*The key to happiness belongs
to everyone on earth
who recognizes simple things
as treasures of great worth.*

AUTHOR UNKNOWN

Then Came Annie

BY DEE ABRAMS

How I'd prayed I'd be a grandma! All my life I'd wanted children—and grandchildren. My beloved husband, Arthur, and I hadn't been able to have kids, and when he died I felt so alone. Sure, I had friends. But it wasn't the same. There was no daughter to call to fuss with over an old family recipe. No son to be proud of. Arthur's children from his previous marriage dropped out of my life after his death. All I had left of my step-grandchildren was an old photo album. I'd buried it in a closet after not seeing or hearing from them for years. But I couldn't bury my broken heart.

Then one day the phone rang. "I'm from the foster grandparents' program at Ruth Rales Jewish Family Service," the caller said. Several weeks earlier, as much out of loneliness as charity, I'd volunteered to be paired with a child needing a grandparent. I'd done it somewhat hesitantly. Now my heart raced. "We have a match for you," the woman said. "Her name is Annie, and she's three."

"That's wonderful!" I said. Still, a part of me hesitated.

"Just meet her," the woman urged. "Her mother is divorced, and it's just the two of them. No other family. Annie could really use someone else in her life."

No other family. I knew how that felt. "Okay," I said. "I'll try." I spent the rest of the day preparing for our meeting. *I don't know if I can do this*, I thought. How do you entertain a three-year-old?

Stories! I drove to the local bookstore where I saw *Miss Spider's Tea Party*. I snatched it up. That had been one of my step-grandchildren's favorites!

I went to the community center to meet Annie. She wasn't anything like I'd imagined. She had beautiful ebony skin and black, tightly curled hair. The woman hadn't told me that Annie's mother was Jewish and her father African-American. But that didn't faze me. What got me was her smile. So innocent, so trusting. It put me completely at ease.

"Hi, Annie," I said. "My name is Dee. Would you like me to read to you?" Her eyes lit up. She led me to two chairs across the room. I opened the book and began to read. I felt her cheek brush against my arm.

"That's Miss Spider!" she said, pointing. By the last page, I thought, *Maybe this can work.*

I closed the book when another woman entered the room. "I'm Barbara, Annie's mother," she told me. "You two seem to have hit it off." She pulled me aside and said, "Annie is turning four next week. Would you like to come to her party?"

Memories of my step-grandchildren came rushing back. That photo album in the closet was stuffed full of pictures of birthday parties over the years. I thought we'd been so happy. But after Arthur died, my birthday cards and letters to them came back marked, "Moved. No forwarding address." Did I really want to get attached to another child who'd walk out of my life? I glanced over at Annie. That smile of hers.... "I'd love to come," I said.

The party was at a park. A dozen kids ate cake, played on the swings, and sang. Annie had such fun with her friends. So much so that it felt as if I were invisible. *What are you doing here?* I wondered. *Annie doesn't need you. Not like you thought.*

But I couldn't keep away from her. I asked Barb if I could take Annie to a local arts festival. "She'd love that," Barb said.

The art festival was packed. "Hold my hand," I said. "I don't want to lose you." Annie slipped her tiny hand into mine. A tingle went through me.

At one of the booths a woman was painting children's faces. "Can I get a butterfly?" Annie asked.

"Of course you can." I reached into my purse and pulled out the camera I had brought along. "As long as I can take your picture. I want to make a scrapbook."

Annie agreed. While the woman painted the butterfly on Annie's face, I snapped picture after picture.

I hated having to drop her off at home.

Right before Annie ran inside, she gave me a big hug and a kiss. "Can I call you Grandma?" she asked.

I took at least one picture of Annie every time we met after that day. I'd get double sets—one for me and one for Annie.

"Why don't you come for dinner on Friday?" Barb asked one afternoon. She made an excellent roast chicken with vegetables.

After we ate, Barb lit some candles and said a prayer in Hebrew. I closed my eyes and silently said a prayer of my own.

I adopted Annie and Barb as fully as they adopted me. Many a Friday I had dinner with them. I was there when Barb remarried a wonderful man named Gordie. I was at the hospital when she gave birth to Leah, and then to Noa.

Yet after eight-and-a-half years, there are still days I fear Annie's leaving me behind. She's thirteen now. *How long will she want to hang around with me?* I wonder.

It's at times like these that I remember visiting Annie and Barb one day. Annie had grabbed my hand and said, "Grandma, Mommy and I have a big surprise for you." From behind her back she'd pulled a thick book. The cover read, "A Book about Grandma Dee and Me."

I took it in both hands and sat down. Page after page was filled with photos of Annie, or Annie and me. She'd made a photo album too! At the end of the book she'd pasted a crayon drawing of a child and a woman holding hands. "From your loving grand-daughter," it read. "Forever."

A Second Chance

I always wondered how the fact would feel—
To be a grandmother! Oh, others
Had boasted of it—but I scarcely believed
That they were truly thrilled with hope again.
But now I, too...feel strong, renewed—
As if my hands, which, numb,
Clung futilely to life had gained fresh grasp.
I've laid a lien on ages still to come!

T. COGSWELL

She Was Running My Household!

BY JEAN JEFFERSON

Perhaps the trouble between my mother-in-law and me would never have happened if David and I had been married a little longer before his mother came to live with us. It was just at the time when a young wife needs to develop her own methods of keeping house and raising children, though, that Grandma came. With Grandma there was only one method of making a bed, seasoning a stew, or conducting a life.

At first it was like a happy visit. I was so awkward and she so experienced. I really did admire her. She had raised her own family against tremendous physical and financial hardships. There was a tireless quality in the way she attacked dirt before it was settled. She canned enough food for a ten-year famine and then began mending whenever she sat to rest. I used to think, I'm seeing the kind of strength that made pioneer women.

The trouble was that the visit did not end. Grandma remained and applied her strength to running my household, raising my children, and managing my social life! David kept out of it, deeply involved in his job.

The only explanation I can find for accepting the situation was my own mistaken ideas about love. I'd been brought up to know that a Christian puts others before self. Gentleness, patience, mildness, forgiveness—these were what the word "Christian" meant to me.

When I first began to resent Grandma's interference in our lives, I fought down the anger within as I would have fought the devil himself. My whole effort around the house was to keep the peace. If Grandma found fault with something, I apologized. If she contradicted, I sought a compromise, If she raised her voice, mine grew softer. The angrier I got about everything, the harder I tried to be kind and to disguise my anger from myself.

I suppose this state of affairs might have gone on forever, if I hadn't finally seen the damage it was doing to our children. Grandma often countermanded my instructions to Janie and Paul, and I knew the children were confused.

As they grew older, however, their confusion changed to indifference. When I spoke they often paid no attention. In an effort to be obeyed, I'd end up screaming at them. Then I would make up for it by reversing my order and giving in. The more my self-confidence faltered, the more violent became the scenes between the children and me, and the more plausible Grandma's claim that I was an incompetent mother and that she was the only one who could manage them.

I'd crawl into bed each night appalled at the way I'd acted, frightened by the ugly feelings inside me. I really hated Grandma now and could no longer hide the truth from myself.

One night after an especially difficult session trying to get my nine-year-old boy to bed, I went into my bedroom and shut the door. I was ashamed and defeated and felt utterly helpless.

If it's like this now when he's little, I thought, *what will it be like when he's a teenager!*

Sudden overwhelming fear for my son drove me to my knees beside the bed. My face pressed against the bedspread, I simply cried out in desperation, "God, help me!"

Unbelievable as it sounds, I do not think that before that moment I had ever asked Him for help. My prayer life had been a kind of bootstrap attempt to lift myself to Christlike heights of dutiful behavior.

But I could not rise that high. I was begging Him now to come to me. To my joy He came, first as a stillness, quieting my fears, my tensions, and my anger. As He emerged, I found no condemning Presence, but a blinding, challenging love. I seemed to be a drop of water carried along in an ocean of love. That love was not only for me, but for Grandma, my children, my husband; for all.

Strange—but I always had thought of love as a soft, pliable thing, but here was something firm and bracing beyond anything I'd ever experienced. The first demand of this love was to set things right with a child.

I rose from my knees, went to Paul's room, and sat down on his bed. As he reached a small hand toward mine I thought, *God has been here too, and smoothed the way.*

Very softly, with tenderness I really felt, I said, "This is no way for a mother and her little boy to act." In the silence I felt the slight pressure of his hand in mine. "We are going to find a way to be happy together. I don't know how, but I know we will."

Leaning over to kiss him, I heard a murmur, "I love you, Mommy."

During the next few weeks, my self-assurance grew. *No more peace in the place of love*, I thought one morning surveying the scene after we finished breakfast.

Grandma stood at the sink swishing dishes through the sudsy water.

"Paul says you are thinking of having Mrs. Forsyth give him piano lessons," she began.

"That's right, Grandma. Paul's schoolteacher thinks he may have real talent in music."

"Nonsense!" Grandma plunged a pot into the suds. "Boys don't care anything about music. They want to play baseball. Paul's going to make Little League this spring.

Then, catching sight of Paul coming down the stairs, she said, "You don't really want to study piano, do you, Paul?"

Paul looked at Grandma, then at me. "Gee, Mom, I don't want to give up baseball."

"Nobody's suggesting it," I said.

"Well, he certainly couldn't do both," said Grandma, her chin jutting ominously. "Don't be ridiculous, Jean. Let him enjoy his youth!"

"Paul, you go on to school. We'll talk this over later." As Paul ran out the door I tried to steady the fluttery feeling in my stomach. "Grandma, sit down and have a cup of coffee with me." I took down two clean cups and started to fill them. She looked at me suspiciously, wiped her hands, and sat down.

"Grandma, the matter of whether or not Paul takes piano lessons—that's something for Paul, David, and me to decide, isn't it?" My eyes held hers firmly.

"My opinions don't count, I suppose! Why, I feel about those children as though they were my own!"

"I know you do, Grandma. Unfortunately, I've been a little confused about it too. But no more. David and I love you, Grandma, and we want you to feel welcome in our home. But from here on we will make the decisions about Paul and Jane. I'm asking you to respect our decisions even when you don't agree with them."

For once, Grandma was stunned into speechlessness. The strength of my words somewhat overwhelmed me too. Yet beneath it all was the curious feeling that Grandma welcomed this speech of mine.

As it turned out, finding my proper role helped Grandma find hers. Perhaps she had never known a way to be loved except by being needed. In time she discovered that she could sit in a chair without a pile of mending and still be valued—valued for herself. I think David always had been a little in awe of her strength as a mother. Now, bit by bit, he had the joy of discovering her as a person.

Once Grandma stopped competing for the role of parent to Paul and Jane, she became that infinitely special someone—their grandmother. No longer responsible for discipline, she became their confidante, companion, and ally.

As for Grandma and me, we achieved a kind of friendship the only way friendships are ever formed—by being ourselves. Oh, I don't mean that God instantly removed all friction between us. We clashed on numerous occasions after that morning, and I was not always so bold. But that day saw the beginning of a long step forward in my Christian walk.

Somehow in Christ's command to love one's neighbor I had never heard the words "as thyself." But I was learning that until we find and really know ourselves, we cannot possibly achieve the real relationships God intends for us to have with those around us.

The Way of Love

"Teacher, which is the great commandment in the law?" Jesus said to him, "'You shall love the Lord your God with all your heart, with all your soul, and with all your mind.' This is the first and great commandment. And the second is like it: 'You shall love your neighbor as yourself.'"

MATTHEW 22:36–39 NKJV

Split-Level Family

BY AMANDA SAFIRSTEIN

When my son Jack first put the question to my husband and me, I gaped for a moment, speechless. *Oh, please, God, I thought, don't let me say the wrong thing.* I chose my words carefully.

"I'm glad you and Sue feel you'd like to live with us while she goes back to college for her master's. But would moving in here with your father and me be wise? Perhaps a nearby apartment might be better." All the unpleasant tales of two women under one roof raced through my mind.

"No, Mom, we figured it all out. We could pay for Sue's tuition and books with the money we'd save by staying here. We could send Eliot to preschool, and Sue could count on you in an emergency. What do you say?"

"Of course! What's the big deal?" Sam, my husband, interjected. "Move in any time you like."

I glanced at Sam, then nodded. "If you're sure it's what you and Sue want."

Jack hugged me. "I told Sue you'd say yes. Gee, thanks, Mom."

When friends and relatives learned the news, their chorus of misgivings sent chilling doubts through me. "You'll wreck the nice relationship with your daughter-in-law," they groaned. Over and over they told me, "You'll be sorry."

How can they be so sure, I wondered. Why would two families under one roof have to be misery? Didn't the psalmists of my people sing about the joys of families living together in harmony?

I remembered their words: "Behold...how pleasant it is for brethren to dwell together in unity!" I remembered the song we sang together during the holidays: "*Ma tovu chaleha Yaakov,*" that is, "How goodly are thy tents, O Israel."

Torn by conflicting urges, I phoned Sue. "Dear, everyone says that two families living together won't work."

"If your friends say such things, Mom, can you imagine what mine tell me? But we still want to come."

I swallowed deeply. "Okay, hon."

One of the poets said, "The loving are the daring." I hoped we weren't daring too much, but just maybe we could prove the psalmist right and our friends wrong.

Well, faith and hope are a good basis, I thought, *but there have to be some practical things I can do to reduce the chances of friction between us.*

I knew, for example, we could provide for Jack and Sue's privacy. Our split-level house has a kitchen, living room, two bedrooms, and two baths on one level. A flight of steps and a door lead to a large recreation room and bathroom downstairs. Three more steps down leads to the basement with laundry facilities.

Bathroom facilities would have to be shared. But it would be possible to make separate living areas by putting Jack and Sue on the lower level.

Sue and Jack were delighted with the idea. "Oh, Mom," Sue exclaimed, "it'll be wonderful to have the backyard so handy for Eliot to play in."

Jack spent the following weekend partitioning the recreation room into two areas. His results looked so good that I asked Sam to shop for kitchen appliances as a surprise for Sue. We found a good, used refrigerator, a stove, and a dishwasher, all priced right.

"We're here, Grandma. We're here!" Eliot shouted as their van drew up. In no time their possessions were in place. Sound system and desk, sofa and comfortable chair completed the illusion of a small but pleasant living room. Eliot's furniture fit the storage closet as though built to order, as did the bedroom things for the area Jack had partitioned.

Seeing Sue's joy when she saw the kitchen we had created for her was the best of all. Tears welled up in her lovely blue eyes. "Thank you, Mother. You'll see. You'll be glad you took us in." It was enough then just to thank God, silently, that we were off to a good start.

Those first few weeks were full of learning situations for all of us—learning to keep the driveway clear, to share the phone, to share the bathroom, to consult on meal planning and shopping, and to respect each other's privacy. That last part was the hardest of all. Often I was glad we had the door between us. I knew Sue was too.

The kitchen proved a stroke of divine inspiration. Sue could be a housewife or let me head up the culinary department. When she chose to share my kitchen, I knew it was because she wanted to, rather than because she had to. That made sharing fun. We grandparents got an extra dividend. Bursting with pride, Eliot would take us by the hand. "Come. You're to eat downstairs at my house today."

The first cold day, however, we had our first flare-up.

"Shut the windows. Put a sweater on Eliot. Turn up the heat." Sam gave Sue a dozen rapid-fire orders. I, no smarter than he, added my bit as well.

By nightfall, Eliot was willful and disobedient. To discipline him, Sue said, "No TV tonight."

"Darling," I called down the stairs to the four-year-old, "come up here. You can watch it with Grandpa and me."

Blue eyes flashing with held-back tears, Sue almost yelled, "I said he was to have no television!"

Her voice brought me to my senses, I tell you. I cornered Jack later. "You know us better than Sue does," I began. "We don't mean to interfere."

"I know, Mom," Jack said. "But Sue's afraid Dad will be hurt if she doesn't follow his suggestions. She doesn't know how you'd react either."

"You tell Sue to be firm—and friendly. We'll straighten out. And, Jack, always feel free to put into words what she might hesitate to say. Promise?"

"It's a deal," Jack said happily. "Now, do me a favor too. Get Dad to accept our share for the utilities."

"I'll do it," I agreed.

Next came the babysitting problem. We understood why our kids assumed, as long as we were home anyway, we were ideal babysitters. It didn't work out that way. We couldn't sleep for fear we wouldn't hear Eliot downstairs. Jack rigged up an intercom, but all it did was make me run up and down stairs to be sure it was working.

One day I took my own advice not to let a small problem become a big one. "Sue, dear," I said, "the high school has a baby-sitting service. Let's see if we can get one."

"Oh, Mom." Sue's relief was plain. "I wanted to. I was afraid you'd feel hurt."

"I'm glad I found the courage to speak to you!" We both laughed.

Little irritations fester if not dealt with. Other irritations we just had to live with, like clothes scrunched in closets never meant to hold so many or precious objects that weren't snatched away from little fingers in time.

But these were nothing compared to our shared joys. Sue's happy excitement as she told us of Jack's substantial salary raise. Or the glow on my husband's face when Eliot marched upstairs and announced, "I just feel like eating breakfast with you today, Grandpa."

These, and a thousand other precious moments, were ours because we lived together. I'd forgotten the fun of small hands helping to stir a chocolate cake and the smacking of a little boy's lips as he anticipated licking batter from a mixing spoon.

Two years have passed since Jack asked, "May we come?" Whatever it was that friends expected never happened. Instead, we've won their admiration and respect because our family lived together in harmony through our determination to respect one another..

Sue has her master's degree now, and soon they will move into their new home. We were discussing this when Eliot, playing nearby, looked up. "Grandma, are you moving too?" he asked.

"No, honey. You're going to live in your own new house with just Mommy and Daddy."

The young voice struggled to be firm. "But Grandma, why can't you move with us?"

I hugged the boy close and bent to kiss his soft hair. Then Sue's hand touched mine. "Oh, Mom," she murmured, "if you only could."

As my eyes met Sue's, I knew that the circle of love we'd made around us would last throughout our lives.

We had proved the psalmist true. We had dwelt together in peace and found how pleasant it is to share life with the ones we love.

A Circle of Love

Love is a great thing, an altogether good gift, the only thing that makes burdens light and bears all that is hard with ease. It carries a weight without feeling it, and makes all that is bitter sweet and pleasant to the taste.

THOMAS À KEMPIS

Care and Feeding

BY CATHERINE MARSHALL

In the two years I've been a grandmother, I've learned volumes about living in the kingdom of God. Mary Elizabeth is able to slip up on my blind side with her teaching since she bears no resemblance to a prophet or dominie. Large, round blue eyes and a piquant nose are framed by blond hair like her mother Edith's. At two, she has sturdy, well-formed legs that carry her into the most unlikely places, a disarming smile with a touch of coyness, and a way of pronouncing yes and no that makes her sound like a charter member of the Women's Liberation Movement.

What this child does to our household is remarkable. My writing schedule is forgotten while Mary Elizabeth and I enjoy a tea party, using tiny blue china cups acquired just for this occasion. Her Uncle Jeffrey, age fifteen, has no objection to becoming a babysitter. He never walks Mary Elizabeth around the block in her stroller; he races her while she chortles. And you should just see her flirting with her grandpa, the executive editor of Guideposts—or better, see him drop down on all fours to bray like a donkey and kick his heels in the air.

All of this adds up to joy. We watch Mary Elizabeth awaken each morning to a world full of wonders. What has become commonplace to us adults still has the freshness of surprise for her. The flying birds, the cloud formations, cows seen in a field, a flower, fragrances, food over which to smack the lips, the rhythm of nursery rhymes and poetry, music—all fill her with excitement.

And like any normal child, she expresses what she feels immediately, exuberantly, without self-consciousness. Her rag doll Muffin had lost her painted-on eyes, nose, and mouth in the washing machine. While Mary Elizabeth slept one night, I replaced Muffin's missing features. When this little girl woke to find that Muffin again had a face, she kissed the doll's new eyes over and over in an ecstasy of recognition—while I marveled, not at her open delight, but at my own restraint. How often I too, have felt my heart jump for joy at the sight of a well-loved face after an absence. How inadequate my, "It's nice to see you again."

Through Mary Elizabeth I have been reminded of Christ's extraordinary statement, "Except ye...become as little children, ye shall not enter into the kingdom of Heaven." I begin to understand why Jesus was careful to specify the diminutive "little children." These very tiny ones are still fresh from the hand of their Maker, children who have not yet had time to absorb the prejudices, resentments, social distinctions, and cruelties we grown-ups mistakenly call "wisdom."

In my reading recently, I have come across descriptions of how adults feel when they enter the kingdom of God through what Jesus called "the new birth." Interestingly, what they experience is almost identical with what we watch in Mary Elizabeth. This is how one woman describes it:

I cannot say exactly what the mysterious change was. I saw no new thing, but I saw all the usual things in a miraculous new light, in what I believe is their true light. Every human being, every sparrow that flew, every branch tossing in the wind, was caught in and was a part of the whole mad ecstasy of loveliness, of joy, of importance, of intoxication of life.

It made me think of Mary Elizabeth's father, Peter John Marshall, at age five, standing with his nose pressed against the windowpane, laughing with glee at the fireworks of an autumn thunderstorm. "Mommy," he'd said, "the lightning looks like string beans dancing."

Another aspect of this springtime of life—almost as if small children were back in the Garden of Eden—is that Mary Elizabeth feels the necessity of naming every living creature around her. She was not really at home during her first visit to our Florida setting until she had decided upon names acceptable to her. Thus Mary, who helps us keep house, became "Yehh-yehh"—usually enunciated as lustily as if Mary Elizabeth were rooting for the Braves. Great-grandmother (the original Christy) is tagged "Na-na." I am invariably "Mygandma." Her grandpa Len is "Popi." Last Christmas before Mary Elizabeth could manage two-syllable words, Jesus became the "Baby Zoohpff," and I believe that He heartily approved.

Oddly, this naming task was one of the first functions that God gave to the original man Adam. "The Lord God formed every beast of the field and every bird of the air, and brought them to the man to see what he would call them."

Another reality of Eden was tender love among living things. We grown-ups have only to watch little children to realize how callused we have become.

Among Mary Elizabeth's favorite books is one of the nursery rhymes set to music. One day her mother sang to her:

Rock-a-bye baby in the treetop
When the wind blows the cradle will rock.
When the bough breaks the cradle will fall
And down will come baby, cradle and all.

Edith was startled to have her daughter burst into tears. Then she understood—Mary Elizabeth was crying because the baby had fallen down. Since the tears were genuine, Edith made a story of how daddy had come and had picked up the baby, and kissed her. She explained that the baby was not really hurt at all. That comforted Mary Elizabeth temporarily. But from that day to this, whenever she comes to that page of the book, there is a loud "no!" as she flips over the page.

Nor does the little child have any problem about belief in God. These small ones are still living on the borderline of two worlds. "Train up a child in the way he should go and when he is old, he will not depart from it," goes the familiar verse. Since Jesus said, "I am the way," I am grateful that already our granddaughter is being taught about Him. She doesn't feel happy about going to sleep at night until she shuts her eyes tightly, holds hands with whoever is putting her to bed, and says a happy goodnight to the "Baby Zoohpff."

There was a time when we decided it would be less conspicuous simply to murmur a silent grace while dining out in restaurants. Mary Elizabeth speedily changed that. One night when eight of us were seated at a large round table in the very center of a local restaurant, Mary Elizabeth waited till the food was brought, then shut her eyes tightly, bowed her head, and held out both her hands for the thank-you. And so we had our family grace, holding hands and all, while Jeff said the prayer in the suddenly very quiet room.

The kingdom of God! A realm of love and spontaneity and unabashed delight in God and the wondrous world He made. Jesus told us, "Feed my lambs." This means that we are under orders from Him to give our children the best that we know of His love and understanding. But one little girl has made me wonder if we, after all, are not the ones who get the feeding.

His Generous Gift

Don't you see that children are God's best gift?
The fruit of the womb his generous legacy?

PSALM 127:3 MSG

That's Grandma's Job

BY ALICE CRAWFORD

O n the afternoon before Thanksgiving I stood in a specialty store, fretting over which napkins to buy for our turkey dinner. Choosing them shouldn't have been such a big deal, except that the napkins would be my only contribution to the Thanksgiving celebration at our house. Here I was forty years old, married nineteen years with two teenagers, and I had never cooked a Thanksgiving dinner for my family.

Cooking Thanksgiving dinner had always been my husband, Marvin's, grandmother's job. Since eighty-two-year-old Grandma lived with us, my only responsibility was setting the table. She always cooked the turkey *her* way in *her* turkey roaster with *her* bread-and-celery stuffing and the rest of her menu, which we had eaten every Thanksgiving for nearly as long as I had known Marv.

Now that the kids were getting older, I was beginning to resent this tradition. *I love Grandma, but it's time I started cooking the turkey,* I told myself. I knew most people would relish a day off on Thanksgiving. But in a few short years our kids would be grown and gone. When they looked back on our Thanksgivings together, I feared they wouldn't remember my part in them. With a sigh, I picked napkins decorated with autumn leaves because they reminded me of my childhood Thanksgivings back in New Jersey.

Grandma and Grandpa Crawford had raised Marv in Boise, Idaho. Grandpa had not studied past eighth grade, and Grandma only through ninth. They worked to provide better for Marv. They made sure he went to church, learned to play the piano, and studied hard in school. When Marv graduated from high school, they sent him to Westminster Choir College in Princeton, New Jersey.

I met Marv in the registration line on the first day of school. We both loved music, our churches, and our families. By Christmas we were already talking about marriage, and the following August I flew to Boise to meet Grandma and Grandpa.

I felt more than a little nervous as Marv walked me up to their little frame house on a quiet, shady street. His grandparents peered through the screen door, eagerly anticipating our arrival.

"Hello, Mrs. Crawford," I said to the spunky, petite lady with curly hair and a bright smile.

"You call me Grandma," she insisted right off. And so I did.

Then she sat us down to a huge breakfast. "When you have company, you fix a real meal," she said, eyes twinkling.

From that day, Marv's grandparents became a part of my life. After Marv and I graduated from college and married, they visited often, always fitting in easily, always helping—especially Grandma—with the cooking. They were delighted when our children were born and were even more help.

By the time Grandpa Crawford died, they had moved in with us. Then, when Marv and I got an offer to be ministers of music at a church in Boulder, Colorado, Grandma moved along with us. She made friends in the neighborhood, joined a sewing circle, put in a garden in our backyard, and, of course, produced marvelous dinners for the family from the kitchen in her "quarters."

Every November she pulled out her turkey roaster and started checking the newspapers to find the best prices for fixings. She made a list and planned the same menu: turkey, bread-and-celery dressing, yams, mashed potatoes and gravy, beans from her garden, cranberries, and several pies. One year her thirty-year-old turkey roaster quit working. I assumed we'd cook the turkey in my oven, but she searched all over town until she finally found a new white-enamel turkey roaster.

I glanced at my watch as I pulled into the driveway with my napkins. I didn't have much time to change clothes before Marv and I had to be at the church for the Thanksgiving Eve service. When I entered the front door I could smell the aroma of fresh-baked pies and hear Grandma busying about in her kitchen downstairs. She wouldn't be going to church with us; she'd be clattering around in her fragrant kitchen. A pang of envy mixed in with my resentment.

Sitting down at the piano at church, I felt tense and grumpy, my fingers cold and stiff on the keys. At this service congregants were encouraged to come forward and proclaim their thanksgiving to God. *One thing is for sure,* I thought, *there's no way am I going to give thanks tonight.*

After a few hymns and a homily, people began making their way forward. A shy child thanked God for his parents. A woman for her neighbors during a crisis. A wife for a loving husband.

Then an elderly man slowly shuffled forward and cleared his throat nervously. "We grandparents sometimes have a hard time fitting in and making a contribution to the next generation, but I thank God for my family. They go out of their way to include me. They are the joy of my life because they help me feel worthwhile."

Tears suddenly burned the corners of my eyes as I thought of Grandma's hardworking, selfless way of contributing to our family. How many wonderful dinners her loving hands had prepared for us over the years!

Moments later, I stood before the congregation

"I've been feeling sorry for myself and resentful today because I've never cooked a Thanksgiving dinner for my family. That's always been Grandma's job. But I've been looking at it the wrong way. Grandma isn't trying to take my role away from me; she's trying to give something to our family. So I thank God tonight for Grandma, who contributes so much to our lives."

The next day I took plenty of time setting the table while Grandma put the finishing touches on the turkey and fixings. I got out a crisp tablecloth, our Sunday china, and, of course, my napkins with the autumn leaves. By the time we sat down to say grace, I was filled with thankfulness for Grandma, her turkey, and her comfortably familiar menu. I knew in my heart that when the day comes for me to cook Thanksgiving dinner, I'll do it just the way Grandma always has—turkey roaster and all.

Gratitude for Grandma

Thank You, God, for Grandma;
She gives us all so much.
And thank You for the love
I feel in every word and touch.
Dear God, as I grow older
Help me, too, to see
Life as a gift, to share in love,
And like my Grandma be.

Secret of the Hats

BY LAURA KLASSEN

People who come to my house always notice my grandmother's old hats. They are there for everyone to see, but I mostly keep them as a reminder to myself.

Long before my time, when grandmother was young, she loved to wear hats. Growing up, my sisters and I used them to play dress-up in Granny's back bedroom when we visited. We raided her musty closets and tripped on long, print dresses as we pranced around in her antiquated shoes and oversized costume jewelry. Somehow the props on our heads, old even then, sent our imaginations whirring.

Eventually, when Granny had to be moved into a nursing home, I found myself asking if I could keep her hats. I wasn't sure why. I couldn't have worn any of them even if they had been in style. They were much too small, and time had conspired against them. The two straw hats, once pristine white, sported bows dotted with rust spots. The brim of the cabbage-rose patterned hat had a permanent crimp in back. The black velvet bowler-styled hat sagged across the crown. The camel pillbox, however, though somewhat mashed, had managed to retain an air of austere dignity. Granny must have looked positively sophisticated with the pillbox perched atop her head, as aloof and beautiful as

Jackie Kennedy herself. But of course I had never actually seen that side of Granny.

The Granny I knew was a warm, embracing woman who cooked all day for family gatherings, harvested vegetables from her own garden, devoured Zane Grey novels, and made the world's best fried apple pies. She loved babies and nature, and she reveled in telling stories about being a young wife in the early 1900s, living under the limitless azure sky of Great Falls, Montana.

Though petite, Granny was strong-willed and independent, and for years after Grandpa died she insisted on staying in the big house where she had raised their five children, the youngest of whom is my mother.

When I was grown, I saw Granny only on holidays and at family reunions. Then last summer when I visited her at the nursing home, she didn't know me. Several times she asked my name and my relation to her, groping for some spark of recognition; but it never came. Instead she went on about events and people I didn't know. I listened, trying to be polite, but feeling a sense of awful sadness and futility with every word of our heartbreaking conversation.

For weeks afterward I agonized over that visit. Instead of the precious memories due her, she was living with no history, no emotional ties to family, and no idea what awaited her. Where was God while my grandmother lived with strangers, confused, facing the end of a life of goodness?

I stopped going to church. I wanted no part of a God I didn't understand. Worse, I couldn't bring myself to visit my beloved granny.

Then one afternoon my sadness overwhelmed me. Not knowing what else to do and missing Granny terribly, I gathered her old hats. They still held the faint, familiar odor of Granny's back bedroom. I set the hats in front of me, touching and studying each one as if they somehow held a clue.

I balanced one of the stylish straw hats on my head. I imagined Granny as a girl, energetic and enthusiastic, feisty and carefree, a whole lifetime ahead of her. Even as a grandmother many times over, she still had had the laugh of a schoolgirl.

Wearing the neat pillbox, she had grown into a strong and confident woman. Granny was known in her community for standing up for what she believed in—her family, honesty, and God's infallible goodness.

The smart, sensible cabbage-rose and all-occasion bowler-style hats reminded me that she had been a devoted wife and companion, a dependable friend and neighbor. "Trust God with your burdens, child," she used to say.

I wanted to play dress-up again, but this time I wanted to clothe myself in Granny's qualities. Over the years she had evolved, as women do, her life changing with new priorities. It was time I made a change too—from an impatient young woman demanding explanations from God to one willing to trust His infallible goodness even now, as she did.

Granny's hats were windows through which I saw her, long before my memories of her began and differently from how the world saw her today. Perhaps she was looking out another window, into a future I was too young and naive and healthy to imagine. A future that only a lifetime of loving God prepares one for.

I let my imagination free me from my anger. Instead of the explanations I had demanded, God gave me peace. I was able to trust that God had wonders ahead for my grandmother. He had seen her through a good life and He was with her still, even now. It was time for Granny to put aside the hats of this world, the hats she had worn so well, and to rest.

Not long ago God took Granny home. In my house now, her hats are always on display. Three sit in a glass cabinet in the foyer, and two hang on the wall in a spare bedroom, inviting guests to ask the origin of the collection. "They belonged to my grandmother," I begin proudly. "When she was young, she liked to wear hats..." I wonder if they wear hats in heaven.

Put On Love

Therefore, as God's chosen people, holy and dearly loved, clothe yourselves with compassion, kindness, humility, gentleness and patience.... And over all these virtues put on love, which binds them all together in perfect unity.

COLOSSIANS 3:12, 14 NIV

A Love for the Land

BY LARRY LEWIS

Once I had loved farming, but now I was ready to quit. I was forty-six, raising about 600 acres of corn, soybeans, and hay; and I was dead tired. It was the same treadmill most farmers are on. Pay thousands of dollars for seeds, chemical fertilizers, and pesticides. Work till you drop. Come home smelling like a house tented for termites. Then watch as weather or a bottoming commodities market washes it all away. Get bigger or get out, the agribusiness companies said. I didn't have the money to get bigger. And I didn't know what to do if I got out.

Farming was in my blood. My dad had farmed before he became a postman, and my grandfather and uncles owned small dairies near our house in southwestern New York. From the time I was old enough to handle a pitchfork, I was out baling hay, tending cows, and driving a tractor.

In high school I practically lived on my grandfather's farm. He had heart trouble and needed help with his 400 acres. The farm was beautiful, a few neat fields and a wide expanse of rolling green pasture. High Up my grandfather called it. I'd wake early and listen to the farm stirring. My grandfather would already be weeding the garden before we went to milk the cows. He farmed the old-fashioned way—with hard work and common sense. No fancy technology for him. Just love of the land and an honest, flinty, Depression-era determination to be self-sufficient.

I was determined to live just like him. I majored in agriculture in college then gradually built up my own farm near the small town of Penn Yan, in New York's Finger Lakes region. I worked hard and raised my boys to farm too. But, by the mid-1990s, I was beginning to wonder if I'd made the right choice.

My barns weren't full of the simple tools my grandfather had used. They were stacked with artificial fertilizers so potent they literally burned the soil away. After planting, I spent most of my time spraying pesticides. The companies that sold the chemicals assured farmers they were safe. But a few years before, my neighbor Klaas Martens, who farmed 1,400 acres of corn, soy, and red kidney beans, had lost all movement in his right arm after a blocked nozzle exposed him to a big dose of pesticide.

To top it all off, grain markets seesawed every year. My boys and I could go heavily into debt buying equipment and chemicals, work our tails off, and still lose money.

One day, talking to Klaas, I confessed I was near despair. "Farming is all I've ever done," I said. "But it's killing me. I feel stuck."

"Well," he said slowly, "you could always go organic."

I laughed. After Klaas's pesticide accident, he and his wife, Mary-Howell, had gradually weaned themselves off chemicals and begun selling their grain to organic dairies. Every chance he got, Klaas preached the virtues of organic farming. He and Mary-Howell were no hippies—they went to church and planned to enroll their kids in Future Farmers of America. And I had to admit, their fields didn't look half bad. But organic? It sounded like farming on the fringe to me.

"Try a few acres," Klaas said. "What can it hurt? Think of it as...old-fashioned."

My ears pricked up at those last words, and I agreed to give it a try. I started with thirty acres of red kidney beans, which had done well for Klaas and Mary-Howell. I tilled the soil, planted the seeds, and watched with alarm as, almost immediately, weeds began thrusting up. Ragweed, pig weed, velvet leaf—the field was carpeted with tenacious invaders, all leaching nutrients from the soil and robbing seedlings of sunlight. I panicked and thought about the pesticide in the barn.

"Don't worry," Klaas said. "Weeds are inevitable. You're not going to have those perfect-looking fields you get with chemicals. Run a cultivator to cut some down and, when the beans start coming up, they'll shade the soil and out-compete the weeds. You have to keep on top of it and check the field constantly. But trust me, it'll work."

Run the cultivator. Check the fields. This was a lot more involved than spraying some chemicals and waiting for harvest. Klaas told me I needed to prime the soil too. Artificial fertilizer kills off most of what makes soil naturally good for plants—worms, composting vegetable matter—and replaces it with synthetic nitrogen and other nutrients. Plants get what they need, but the soil goes dead, so that after awhile, nothing will grow in it without more chemicals. Klaas told me I could add ground-up limestone and gypsum to get the balance of acidity and calcium right, then rotate crops to give the soil in each field a chance to rest and recharge.

"You'll get worms going in there pretty soon," he said. "Then you'll have soil plants love."

Hmm, I thought. *Old-fashioned is right. What a lot of work!*

Neighbors came by and saw the weeds sprouting amid the kidney beans. Farmers are sensitive about the look of their fields the way some women are sensitive about their figures. "Are those kidney beans I see in your ragweed field?" they joked. Embarrassed, I mumbled something about worms and life cycles.

Then the beans came in. They were beautiful. And the price! Organic produce, I discovered, could fetch more than twice as much as conventional crops. "I'm going organic," I told Klaas. Of course, it wasn't just the money. It was the satisfaction that came with having produced a crop naturally, the old-fashioned way. Maybe this was how God wanted His land cultivated.

The next year I kept my same crop mixture—corn, winter wheat, soy beans, and various kinds of hay—but planted each without pesticides or artificial fertilizers. The work was intense and nonstop. Grain planting in April. Corn and soy in May. Harvesting grain and winter wheat in summer. Then the hay harvest, followed by corn and soy. Not till November, when I planted the following year's winter wheat, could I rest. There wasn't rest for my mind either. With chemicals, the year is more or less predictable—except for weather. You plant, spray, harvest. Organic farming requires vigilance and perfect timing. Some grains are planted early to shelter later grains from weeds. Fields must be repeatedly cultivated. I couldn't even use poison to kill the rats that fed on my seed supply. I had to trust my cats.

Driving home one late summer evening, watching the sun slide below the lip of a valley, I realized I was exhausted. I had been up since five that morning, doing a little bit of everything. Dragged the cultivator through fields on my thirty-year-old Ford 5000 tractor. Weeded. Tested corn by biting kernels to see if they were dry enough to harvest.

I could have complained. But as I passed a clover field bathed in rich golden light, I realized I was happier than I had been for years. Yes, I was worn out, but worn out the way I had been after a long day on my grandfather's farm. The clover field appeared in the rearview mirror, and I thought, *My fields don't smell like spray anymore. They're beautiful.*

Three years later, my farm was officially certified organic. I practically had to turn customers away. Organic dairies were springing up around New York, and they all needed grain to feed their cows. Around that time Klaas and Mary-Howell bought an old mill in Penn Yan and began grinding organic grain. Customers came calling from New York, Pennsylvania, and Ohio.

It seemed farmers couldn't grow fast enough, and the Martens couldn't grind fast enough, to keep up with demand.

It used to be every transaction with a customer, especially the big agribusiness companies, was merciless bargaining. Now I was working with friends, people I saw in town whose kids I knew. People who were fair. It was Mary-Howell saying hello when I called the mill.

In the winter, when fields were dormant, she and Klaas invited organic farmers in the area to meet once a month to trade advice and help newcomers. The insecurity and competitiveness of my old farming life—the gnawing need to get bigger—was all gone.

Not long ago I was talking to one of my neighbors, a Mennonite farmer named Eddie Horst who milks forty-eight cows and grows the organic grain to feed them on fields down the road. Eddie's wife and eight kids all work on their farm too, and the day I visited, he and one of his older boys were repairing a barn. They put down their hammers, and we talked for awhile about how, in many places, kids are leaving farms, seeking a life that's not a dead end.

"Not here," said Eddie, who even puts his littlest ones to work gathering eggs.

"Not my son either," I said. My youngest son, Matthew, who's twenty-six, farms with me and will probably take over when I retire. I thought back to 1996, when I was ready to quit. How I'd laughed at Klaas's organic proselytizing! In some ways, I guess I have ended up on the fringe—less than one half of one percent of all U.S. farmland is organic. But if that's the fringe, I like it. It's farming the way I remember it. Season to season. Father to son. And, best of all for me, grandfather to grandson.

Pattern of Creation

Whether we are poets or parents or teachers or artists or gardeners, we must start where we are and use what we have. In the process of creation and relationship, what seems mundane and trivial may show itself to be holy, precious, part of a pattern.

LUCI SHAW

Granny's Vegetable Soup

BY MARY LOUISE KITSEN

When I was a little girl, my Granny Lyman made vegetable soup every single Wednesday.

Granny was a widow who supported herself as a dressmaker. Since it was the time of the Great Depression, both Mom and Dad worked long hours in our little florist business to make ends meet. Granny lived with us and did most of the cooking. Granny's vegetable soup, however, was not for her family. She made that soup to give away.

Each Wednesday Granny carefully poured her vegetable soup into large glass jars; and as soon as I arrived home from school, she and I would go out to deliver it. Some of the kids I went to school with laughed about my Wednesday activity. I didn't care one bit. The people we visited were an important part of my childhood.

For example, there was the woman I'll call Charlotte. I had never seen hair like hers before. It was a kind of startling pink. Charlotte wore so much makeup that she looked like a wooden doll. Her two-room apartment was always messy and dirty. Charlotte would take the soup into her kitchen and then come back into the little sitting-bedroom with the jar from the week before.

Granny and I would sit down and listen to Charlotte talk about what might have been if only she'd had some luck. She thought she was an excellent dancer and would have been a movie star too, if only she'd been able to get to Hollywood. Most people laughed at Charlotte behind her back. Not my granny. Granny always heard Charlotte out and then would tell her that she could still make something good of her life.

The visit always ended the same way. Granny would invite Charlotte to join us at church the next Sunday. Charlotte would say she was a sinner and unwelcome in a church.

"God loves you, Charlotte," Granny would say. "You can be forgiven and start new."

One Sunday after the service had just started, Charlotte entered the church. Granny got right up and brought her to sit with us. I could hardly believe it was Charlotte. She didn't have any makeup on ,and her hair was covered by a scarf. It was the start of a new life. Charlotte took a waitress job in a family cafe, and she soon was making a good living; Granny said that her lifestyle had changed for the better.

Then there was Sarah, a God-fearing, black woman who was active in a small church a few blocks from ours. Sarah and her husband had six children, and the salary her husband made as a school janitor didn't go far enough. He had to take on a lot of odd jobs. They never complained. Never asked for charity.

But Sarah did accept Wednesday soup! Two large jars of vegetable soup meant that she could have a good meal without cooking for one night each week. She accepted the soup, and she accepted Granny's offer to look after her children while Sarah went for her weekly walk. Sarah loved her children, but they were a lot of work. She was always knee-deep in noise. For thirty minutes or so, Sarah could go out walking alone. She could enjoy whatever season it was. She could think. Or pray. Wave to her friends. She came back refreshed and ready for another week.

It seemed like a little thing. But not to Sarah.

Then there was Moses, the junkman. What a mess his place was! He had just about anything anyone could want. He had been a widower for many years, and he was bent with age. Everyone said Moses was "tight with a dollar." He lived like a pauper, but they said he had a huge bank account. His sons were lawyers and lived far away from the father and the junkyard that had given them their education.

"Bring my soup, Mrs. Lyman?" Moses would ask.

Granny would give him his jar of soup. He took it, and I cannot recall his ever saying thank you, even though my mom said it was probably the best meal he'd had each week. However, he did always offer Granny her choice of anything in his junkyard.

"Thank you, Moses, but I don't need a thing," Granny would say. "Give it to someone in need."

One day Moses didn't open his door. A neighbor checked the room in the back where he stayed and found Moses had died peacefully in his sleep. Imagine the surprise of everyone (except my granny) when it was discovered that Moses, who was Jewish, had left a large sum of money to a Christian children's home. Granny said that that was his thank-you for the soup.

Our final stop was always at the home of Mrs. Anderson. Mrs. Anderson was a member of our church. She was in her nineties and no longer able to go to church services. Her niece lived with her and took loving care of her. Pastor came to see her each week, and she enjoyed that. But of all the good things in her last years, Mrs. Anderson most enjoyed Granny's visits. The soup and visit meant Mrs. Anderson's niece, like Sarah, could just get away for a little while. And Mrs. Anderson could catch up on the church "gossip."

"The paint in the church nursery is peeling. Can't understand it, because it was only painted last spring."

"Mrs. Paul's boy is home from the Army, and I'm proud to say he has remained a fine Christian young man."

"Karen Miller is going with the Mason boy. I think it's serious, and I'm sure their parents are so pleased."

This was the kind of news Mrs. Anderson missed! Granny made her part of the everyday happenings of the church. Then when her niece came home, Granny and I would say goodbye to Mrs. Anderson and head for home. Another Wednesday was over.

In time Granny became ill with cancer, and her Wednesday trips came to an end. I was eighteen and in college when Granny died. I felt the loss terribly, but I knew she was with God, and that pain could no longer touch her.

When we returned from the cemetery, my mother handed me an envelope with my name written on it in Granny's hand. Inside was a small piece of paper, folded in two. I opened it and found it was Granny's recipe for vegetable soup. But, of course, it was much, much more than that. It was a recipe for living life as a Christian, a legacy left to me by a grandmother who understood people and who loved God.

Love in Action

Dear children, let's not merely say that we love each other; let us show the truth by our actions. Our actions will show that we belong to the truth, so we will be confident when we stand before God

1 JOHN 3:18–19 NLT

Profit Sharing

BY ANTHONY PARKS

P eople sometimes ask me why I do it—why I've given away thousands of shares of stock after all the years I worked to achieve financial success. That's when I tell them about the promise I made when I was growing up in East Oakland, California.

My mother was only sixteen when she had me. To make ends meet, she became a hairdresser and eventually opened her own salon, working early mornings and late nights to get extra customers. I learned to cook and clean so I could help out. The last thing Mom needed after a long day at work was to come home to a load of laundry.

When I was little we lived with my grandmother Naomi, so many of my earliest memories are of her. She made me breakfast in the morning and read to me at night. She took me with her on her housecleaning jobs. She was proud of the work she did and often reminded me, "Always remember that the Bible says that the greatest among you must serve." Many times a friend or neighbor would come over asking for this or that, and my grand-mother always gave whatever she could. Even as a small boy, I knew I wanted to be like her.

At eleven I started working—delivering newspapers, mowing lawns—anything to have a little money of my own. One day I gathered up my earnings and caught a bus to the shopping mall. I bought myself three suits. When I got home, I modeled them for Mom.

"Well, look at you," she said, clapping her hands. "I'm sure you're the only boy in school with three suits. My son, dressed for success!"

When I got to junior high, Mom enrolled me in parochial school. That's where I really began to understand the things in the Bible my grandmother was always going on about. I became the senior altar boy and would wake up at five each morning to serve Mass before going to school. I did it for five months straight. The duties became so routine that I didn't have to even think about them. Instead I thought about God and how best to serve Him. There, amid the dim early-morning rustlings of vestments and the smell of candle wax, I found myself making a silent promise. I would find the talents God had given me and use them to become financially successful. Then I would give to others—to people like my mom, who worked so hard to provide for me, and my grandmother, who was always putting others' needs above her own.

The summer after my freshman year of high school I got my first "real" job, the position of "sweep and mop" at McDonald's. I still remember how excited I was when I graduated to french-fry duty. It was my first promotion. Right then and there I knew that no matter how low on the ladder I had to start, I would climb up. I would work hard, just like Mom, and prove myself.

During high school, I sold vacuum cleaners and cooked at restaurants. My mother and grandmother encouraged me in all my jobs, no matter how unglamorous. Some of my school friends were ending up in jail and worse. Being at a job after school kept me away from trouble.

After graduating, I kept working in the restaurant business. I was quick on my feet and good with people. I took a job at Round Table Pizza and quickly worked my way up the ranks. Other restaurant jobs followed, and it was always the same pattern— waiter, assistant manager, then manager. The hours were long and the money wasn't great. Still I always had the conviction that if I worked hard enough, I would reach my dream of financial success. I was making a list in my head of the people I wanted to give to—family, friends, and people who had given me a chance to show what I could do.

In 1986, I was managing the restaurant at the Sheraton Hotel on Fisherman's Wharf in San Francisco. One morning my mother called and told me that my grandmother had died of a stroke. I felt like I'd had the breath knocked out of me. Suddenly I wasn't sure of anything anymore. My grandmother was everything to me. How would I achieve my goals without her? I fumbled onward, mechanically carrying out my responsibilities each day, lost in a fog of grief. But it was as if I kept hearing Grandmother asking me what I'd done for others. My drive to succeed stirred within me again and grew stronger than ever. I had to go on, so I could fulfill the promise I'd made to help people, the promise inspired by the lessons my grandmother had taught me.

Not long after, a former supervisor of mine at the Sheraton, Steve Wiezbowski, asked me to become assistant manager of Neptune's Palace, one of his restaurants on the pier. I leaped at the offer. After only a few months, the general manager position opened up. I told Steve I wanted it.

"I know I've never managed a restaurant this size before," I said, "but I can do this job. I'm sure of it."

Steve regarded me thoughtfully. "Then you've got your chance," he said. "I'll give you ninety days to prove yourself, but if you don't, you can't go back to being assistant manager— you're out."

That lit a fire under me. *Stand back and watch me work*, I thought. I read books, took business courses, and worked harder than I ever had in my life. Steve was always ready to answer questions and offer advice. I ate, breathed, dreamed my job, and at the end of ninety days, it was mine for good. For the first time, I was in charge of a staff of over one hundred people.

Soon I became director of operations for several restaurants owned by the same company. But after seven years there my dream seemed to stall.

Lord, are you telling me to move on? I asked. I sensed the answer was yes, so I walked away. Without another job in hand, I left

Neptune's Palace in 1994 to see what else was out there—but not before I added Steve to that list I was making in my head.

Recruiters called with some good offers; I took the one that offered the most opportunity for me to make a big impact. It was for what was then a small chain of coffee shops called Starbucks. I opened its first San Francisco stores and co-authored the company's diversity-awareness program. By 1996, of course, Starbucks was huge, and again I longed for a new project to sink my teeth into.

Everywhere I turned I heard about the Internet, the tremendous possibilities the web revolution offered. I wanted to be part of it, though I had no college degree and no technology background. I had come to see, though, that sometimes in life you have to step back to move forward. I would break into this new industry, even if I had to start out cleaning computer screens.

Everyone was calling the dot-com frenzy the new gold rush. That got me thinking. I did some reading about the real Gold Rush and realized it wasn't just the people who found gold who struck it rich—it was also the people who sold picks and shovels to the gold miners, the folks who served a need. I decided to use my twenty-two years of customer service experience to start a business specializing in customer service for technology companies.

The company didn't make much money, but it did get noticed. I got a call from a recruiter about a new venture that Louis Borders, the founder of Borders bookstores, was planning. It eventually developed into an online grocery store called Webvan. Intrigued by the concept, I signed on as head of customer service, one of eight people to start the company.

After a lifetime working in restaurants, computers took some getting used to. But I loved being part of something new and innovative. By the time I left Webvan at age forty to pursue my own projects, I felt like a new man. I had finally stopped climbing other people's ladders and built my own instead.

One November day I got a call from the CFO of Webvan. "We go public next week," he told me. "You'll be getting around half a million shares." I thanked him and put down the phone. *It's finally happened,* I thought. I got a pen and piece of paper. I sat down at my desk and wrote out the list I'd waited almost thirty years to make. Five hundred shares to one, a thousand to another—the list kept growing. I began taking it with me wherever I went, adding more names as I thought of them.

Some were people I hadn't talked to in years, but mostly they were friends like Bernadette Robertson and Laurie Reemsnyder. Both are single mothers working hard, just like my mother did, to make a better life for their kids. Some were people I wanted to thank like Steve Wiezbowski, who helped me push myself to excel. Others were people I wanted to encourage, like Mario Gonzalez, a Mexican immigrant who started as a janitor and worked his way up to banquet manager at Neptune's Palace. And, of course, there was my mom who, like my grandma, showed me what hard work is all about.

Each time I give away shares, I get a feeling even more satisfying than when I got my first promotion at McDonald's. I am grateful for the dream God put in my heart so many years ago, the promise He moved me to make. Like I said, people sometimes ask me why I'm giving away what I've worked so hard to achieve. All I know is that every time I give away shares of my wealth, I feel richer.

Gifts Returned

Give, and it will be given to you. A good measure, pressed down, shaken together and running over, will be poured into your lap. For with the measure you use, it will be measured to you.

LUKE 6:38 NIV

Bubba

BY BERT CLOMPUS

I was about five when I first realized that *Bubba*—Yiddish for "grandmother"—was not on good terms with Mom. Whenever Dad drove us to Harrisburg, Pennsylvania, to visit his mother, it was always the same story. If Bubba spoke to Mom at all, her words were clipped and cold.

On one visit Mom and Bubba were washing the dinner dishes when a teacup slipped out of Mom's hands and shattered on the floor. A look of disdain clouded Bubba's broad face. "Mollie," she grumbled, "you never were good enough for my son!"

I was shocked. How could Bubba talk like that? My eyes welled with tears as I watched Mom bite her lip and look to Dad. He was red-faced and wordless.

My grandfather's eyes blazed at Bubba and he spoke up. "You apologize to Mollie!" Grandfather demanded. Bubba, a large woman who dwarfed my short and wiry grandfather, merely folded her arms and pursed her lips stubbornly.

Our visit ended abruptly but not before my grandfather steered me down the steps of the small apartment to his grocery store below. He slid open the door at the back of the candy case. "Here, Bert, take one," he said, as if the sweetness could purge the bitter aftertaste of Bubba's outburst. I shook my head, then relented, selecting a cherry sour ball.

I was still rolling it around in my mouth and resisting the urge to bite into it as we drove home. Mom must have been doing the same thing with Bubba's words, rolling them around in her mind and fighting the urge to complain to Dad. About the time I finally crunched the sour ball, Mom blurted out, "Ike, why didn't you say something?"

Dad didn't answer. He only gripped the steering wheel a little tighter and drove a little faster. At last Mom cried out, "So is that what you think too? I'm not good enough?" I was nearly thrown off the backseat as Dad slammed on the brake pedal and swerved to a stop on the shoulder of the road. "How can you say that, Mollie?" he gasped, grabbing her hand.

"I know I had only a third-grade education when I came to this country," Mom sobbed. "I know I had to sew in a sweatshop to help support my family. I know you are your mother's favorite son. But does that make me not good enough, Ike?"

My father's face, usually so stern, softened. "Are you through?" he asked quietly. "I think you already know the answer, Mollie."

Mom nodded, rummaging in her purse for a tissue. Their eyes finally met and Dad kissed his fingertips and touched them softly to Mom's lips. I knew things were all right again. But I also knew how Dad felt, torn between the two women he loved most in the world, not wanting to hurt either one.

The next time we went to Harrisburg, Mom insisted on waiting in the car while we visited with Bubba.

"I'm staying with Mom," I declared loyally.

"Go with your father, Bert," Mom ordered.

"All right," I said, giving in, "but I'm not speaking to Bubba."

Bubba pretended to be disappointed that Mom wasn't with us. When she smiled and spread her huge arms wide for me, my resolve evaporated. I melted, all the while feeling like a traitor. But what five-year-old can resist a grandmother's hug? When Dad and my grandfather went downstairs to the store, I mustered my courage and asked Bubba why she didn't love Mom. She refused to answer.

"But you love me, don't you?" I persisted.

Bubba pulled me onto her lap. "Sure I do!" she said fiercely.

"Well, if you love me, why can't you be nice to Mom?"

Bubba shrugged. "It's different," she said, "and you're too young to understand." Just then Dad came upstairs and said it was time to leave.

Not long after, Bubba took ill with a severe case of the flu. Stubborn as always, she refused to go to the hospital or stay with any of her children nearby. My grandfather had his hands full working twelve-hour days tending the store, so my dad offered to bring Bubba to recuperate with us, in the home of her favorite son. To my surprise, Mom agreed. My stomach knotted at the prospect of the two of them under one roof. How would they be able to get along in such close quarters?

The next day Dad followed Bubba into the house, carrying a battered brown valise and a large paper bag. He put the bag on the kitchen table.

"What's this?" Mom asked.

"I brought my own food," said Bubba, punctuating her statement with a series of hacking coughs.

Mom emptied the bag of its contents: a large jar of pickles, a large jar of sauerkraut, and six cans of store-bought chicken soup. "This isn't food for a sick person," Mom said, glancing dismissively at Bubba. The tension between them made my knees weak.

Lord, I prayed desperately, please let them get along just this once. Please.

"I'll get Bubba settled in the guest room," Dad interjected quickly, taking my grandmother by the arm.

"She's not eating this food, Ike!" Mom called after them.

"I will too!" Bubba coughed.

"I don't want her dying in my house!"

"I wouldn't dream of it, Mollie!"

"Both of you—that's enough!" Dad shouted, pulling Bubba up the stairs. When he returned he took Mom aside. "You've got to try to show my mother respect while she's in this house," he whispered hoarsely. Then he stomped off to work.

Red-faced, silent, and muttering a prayer, Mom swept aside Bubba's groceries, and went to work herself—chopping and slicing to prepare a big pot of her homemade chicken soup. While the glorious concoction bubbled and simmered on the stove, Mom baked a fresh loaf of challah—the sweet braided bread she usually made for the Sabbath. When it was all done she fixed a tray with her best china and carried it up to Bubba. There was something almost defiant about her as she climbed the stairs.

I tiptoed behind and watched Mom silently hand Bubba the tray. There was a long nerve-racking pause before Bubba croaked, "For me?" Mom didn't answer. Instead she briskly smoothed the covers on Bubba's bed and left.

Downstairs I asked Mom why she had gone to such trouble for Bubba. "I thought challah and soup was just for Fridays? I mean, Bubba isn't even nice to you."

"That doesn't matter, Bert," she said. "She's still your father's mother, and she's still my guest. That's how we'll treat her; apparently that's what God wants."

Later I went up to get Bubba's dishes. "Isn't Mom's chicken soup the best?" I asked her.

Bubba hemmed and hawed and shifted in bed. "It's not half bad," she finally admitted, as if the words were torture to get out.

"Mom," I said, handing her the tray downstairs, "Bubba said your chicken soup is the best."

"She did?" Mom said, failing to mask her surprise. This was high praise coming from Bubba, and I thought Mom straightened a little bit with pride.

Every day from then on, Mom made Bubba soup and fresh challah and served it on her best dishes. It was good medicine, and not just for Bubba's flu. Each time Mom took Bubba her tray, they lingered together a little longer. One afternoon, while I listened outside the door, I heard Bubba say, "Mollie, I have six daughters and not one of them makes chicken soup to match yours."

"Oh, go on, Bubba," said Mom modestly. "Can I get you some more?"

I peeked into the room just in time to see Bubba raise herself from bed and give Mom a good long hug. I knew how that felt.

Mom was blushing when she came out and scooted me away. But later she took me by the shoulders and said, "Bert, if I grumble about the girl you marry, just tell her to keep trying to love me anyway. God will do the rest."

I think Bubba stayed on a few days extra just because she was having a good time. Seeing his wife and mother get along at last lifted a huge burden from my father. And I was glad God had heard my prayer and helped bring Mom and Bubba together.

If we treat one another with respect and love, even if it's difficult, He'll look after the rest. That's what the two women I loved most in the world taught me when I was five years old.

I Wish You Love

I wish you love, and strength,
and faith, and wisdom,
Goods, gold enough to help some needy one.
I wish you songs, but also blessed silence,
And God's sweet peace when every day is done.

DOROTHY MACDONALD

A Note from the Editors

Guideposts, a nonprofit organization, touches millions of lives every day through products and services that inspire, encourage, and uplift. Our magazines, books, prayer network, and outreach programs help people connect their faith-filled values to their daily lives. To learn more, visit Guideposts.org or GuidepostsFoundation.org.